STEVEN J. APTER

Personal Growth

THE STRUGGLE FOR IDENTITY
AND HUMAN VALUES

Clark Moustakas
THE MERRILL-PALMER INSTITUTE
DETROIT, MICHIGAN

HOWARD A. DOYLE PUBLISHING COMPANY
Cambridge, Massachusetts 02139

Second Printing - 1971

Library of Congress Catalog Card Number 76-79235

PERSONAL GROWTH

Copyright © 1969 by Clark Moustakas. Printed in the United States of America. All rights reserved. This book, or parts thereof, may not be reproduced in any form without permission of the publishers.

For

Subudhi and Helen

*where human expressions and ethical
values connect and intertwine
in common fate and destiny*

Contents

Foreword by Eugene D. Alexander

Chapter 1. Alienation, Education and Existential Life — 1

Chapter 2. Creativity and Conformity in Education — 27

Chapter 3. The Authentic Self: The Readiness to Be — 38

Chapter 4. Authentic and Unauthentic Learning — 47

Chapter 5. Essential Conditions in the Development of the Self — 66

Chapter 6. The Confrontation of Two Brothers — 80

Chapter 7. The Burden of Sensitivity and Compassion — 94

Acknowledgments

I express my appreciation to the many persons who helped me to create *Personal Growth:* the teachers, principals, and counselors in my seminars in human relations in the school systems in Metropolitan Detroit; the graduate students in my course, Personal Growth and Psychological Counseling; the children and adolescents with whom I have met deeply and intimately in individual therapy sessions; the children in elementary schools who have shared their essays and poems with me. I also thank my children, Bob, Wendy, Kerry, Steve, and Beth, each of whom in his own way has insisted on freedom and authenticity in learning and has helped me stay on the path of significant and creative life when I might have strayed toward conventional standards and goals, and my wife, Betty, who stands firmly by human values in learning and living. Further, I wish to recognize The Merrill-Palmer Institute and, specifically, William Rioux, its President, and Irving Sigel, its Research Chairman, for making possible the kind of study this book represents, and Mavis Wolfe for help in its final preparation. I thank, too, Eugene Alexander and Dorothy Lee, who exist significantly in the ideas and values developed in the book.

Foreword

Out of a deep sense of urgency and personal commitment comes this plea for authenticity and encounter in the learning situation. Learning is seen as a living involvement with life, as a commitment to values, as self-searching, as "listening to life." Dr. Moustakas is disturbed by the alienation from life in our schools. He is concerned about the "uniformity of behavior, uniformity of expression, death of individuality, docility, passivity, and conformity" that result from an other-directed curriculum that stresses abstract objective facts at the expense of direct immediate experience. He sees a great gulf between the student and the teacher as each goes his separate way, one to be taught and the other to teach.

In the other-directed school, the child passively absorbs discrete facts programmed for him from a prescribed curriculum. He is judged on his ability to reiterate, organize, and manipulate these facts regardless of their meaning in his life situation or of his particular everyday experiences. The student begins to see himself as one fact among many facts. Brought up under an objectivized curriculum, he tends to observe himself objectively. He sees himself as an object to be manipulated and controlled and, in turn, to direct others. He finds himself disengaged, focusing his whole understanding on his ability to abstract and analyze. In subtle duplicity with the system, the student rejects much of his self that is spontaneous, immediate, and impossible to categorize. He loses connection with his vital inner life processes and becomes a reactive shell responding this way and that to external stimuli. Without an inner core of experienced human values, he seldom is confronted with the deep personal struggle that real learning entails. In the sterile routine progression of preselected, specially graduated subject matter, values are sacrificed for "expediency, efficiency, organization, achievement." The student successfully completes his schooling, perhaps with a superior ranking, at the terrific expense of the personal significance and vital relevance of the entire learning process.

Clark Moustakas contrasts this alienated learning situation with an authentic engagement of the person with life. He stresses learning as a living experience, as a "struggle with life" full of "wonder, excitement, mystery, ecstasy, joy of discovery, meaning of new awareness, love, imagination, inspiration." For real learning, the student must become imbedded in the experience. He must live it, breathe it, feel it, let it find its relevance in the reservoir of all his other vital experiences. The student "must be free to *remain* with that which interests and provokes involvement and collaboration." He must have the freedom to follow it as long as it demands his interests; through nooks and crannies, down winding, treacherous paths, to the crests of mountains, and into the depths of an abyss. Learning, like life, can be joyful; yet, like life, it can also bring pain and sadness. Learning can bring new insights, vital changes, a whole reorganization of beliefs and values. It may lead to a discarding of preconceived ideas, a loss of long-established security, a rejection of once highly valued hopes and goals. The tenuous searching that true commitment to learning entails can be a risky business. It can be fascinating, awesome, shocking. Vital learning becomes a great adventure into the unknown, uncharted, unimagined.

Education transmits the culture to the child. It lets him explore the vast accumulation of man's knowledge. It must also leave him free to "follow his dreams, his imagination, his fantasy." It is out of this infinite melange of personally constructed experience that the new, the creative, the unique emerges. Without this forward thrust into the unknown, there remain only duplication and repetition of the past; just a review of what already has occurred.

In an authentic learning situation, the teacher is not seen as an expert with the answers or as an authority who guides the learner in the right direction. Dr. Moustakas stresses the teacher's relationship with the student as well as the learning role of the teacher. Most important is the teacher's sensitivity and awareness of the student, his ability to encourage the potential and capability of the student, his artfulness in stimulating excitement and inspiration in the student. This can emerge only from dialogue and encounter between teacher and student. By sharing his own self-searching, his own groping struggle to sense and comprehend the universe, the teacher can help develop a living learning situation. The self-assured, well-organized expert in the field, with an authoritative grasp of method and research, can present information and understanding. Yet, without sharing his doubts, his anguish, his joy, there is little vibrancy in the learning situation. Real teaching is not the setting up of preconditions for prescribed goals but rather the creation of experiences that lead to many paths, perceptions, and patterns, experiences that result in unpredictable outcomes. Dr. Moustakas sees the teacher's role as one in which he presents himself in such a way as to say, "Here are materials that have been meaningful to me, here I am, share us." The teacher makes himself available as an open and real person willing to share his vitality in a searching encounter with the student when the student is ready and willing to search with him.

The young child is curious. He is fascinated with everything he sees and touches. He can dash from one new experience to another in awesome excitement. He can dawdle for hours over a single experience, seeing it in ever-new designs and variations. Life is an adventure in learning for him. Then he enters school. Soon learning becomes a drudgery for him. Curiosity turns to conformity. New experiences are avoided as a search is made for the right answer. Learning loses its connection with life.

It is the retention of this natural curiosity, inborn in

all of us, that concerns Moustakas. When professional educators meet, there is much worry and attention focused on motivating the child to learn. Their real interest, however, in the final analysis, is motivating the child to absorb the prescribed stereotype syllabus. In stressing the "authentic self," Dr. Moustakas intimates that it is not necessary to motivate the individual so that he will learn. What is necessary is to free the individual to be his honest, feeling and thinking self. Curiosity and learning are natural components of the real self. If he is true to himself, the individual can do nothing else but learn. Still, he must be free to learn in the direction that self-confirmation leads. Motivation becomes a primary school problem because the teaching situation puts barriers in the way of authenticity and severely restricts the pathways and patterns of learning.

This book is very timely in its reflection of the irritations and unrest on the campus today. At the university level, students are protesting their alienation from their instructors. They complain that their colleges have more the air of an efficient factory than the atmosphere of personal interaction that stirs interest, excitement, and meaning. Students from comfortable, conforming middle-class homes arrive with questions about the significance of life. They look at their parents and wonder about their lack of commitment and their routine pattern of materialistic existence. They grope for new pathways, new values. The find overly objective, overly intellectualized, and, more often than not, conforming professors. They find professors caught up in the prescribed patterns of subject matter and lost in the intricacies of highly involved minor conflicts within the confines of a limited area of a narrow discipline. Frequently, the students themselves become engrossed in the specifics of professional preparation and do not get an opportunity to explore their vital questions about life. Often, they even lose sight of the questions themselves as they fall into the mode of objective scientific disengagement from life. Other students, often the most vital and creative, make the decision to leave the university and meet life directly and honestly in a desperate attempt to discover authentic meaning.

In the high schools the protest is less direct. Students have difficulty paying attention and concentrating on their studies. Some of the brighter ones are observed to be underachieving. There is increased talk of "behavior problems," and the school administrators struggle to develop counseling programs and special curricula to prevent dropouts. Often, students become so involved in absorbing data, concepts, and principles in order to pass examinations that they have little time or inclination for original thinking. Examinations and high marks become most important for the acquisition of that sought-after slot in the highly competitive game of college entrance. The intrinsic goal of learning, itself, gets lost.

The effects of alienation on the elementary school student are even more subtle. The child becomes caught up in the ever-increasing pressure to develop skills earlier and earlier. He very rapidly loses his ability to experience the most highly enriching type of learning situation of all—play. He is told that school is a place for academic work and no nonsense. His natural instinct to use play to examine the unknown, the unexperienced, the felt, the imaginary, is silenced to make way for the implantation of cultural information. He becomes stifled, narrow, unexcited. He is heard to complain about school, how much he doesn't like school. School is too hard, boring, no fun. One is hard put to find a youngster willing to admit that he likes school. School is all work and no play. To give this meaning, it can be rephrased. School is all repetition, reiteration, and no curiosity, imagination, exploration. The elementary school child protests. He cannot put his protestations into abstract terms. But being closer to himself than the older students, he feels it more vitally within. Like a drowning man, he makes a desperate effort to salvage his most significant mode of learning, and recess becomes the most valued period of the day.

Dr. Moustakas speaks for all these young people who

are desperately searching for authenticity and personal integrity. In a highly technological society in which man becomes more and more separated from natural processes and from his own fundamental inner calling, the need to focus on personal growth and spontaneous thinking-feeling becomes imperative. Caught in the segmented static mode of analytic thinking, man has lost his developmental direction. Without connection to the universal formative process of nature, man can make arbitrary choices and decisions that can lead to a rigidification and overspecialization of the species. Concentration on intellectualization is to mankind what the overdevelopment of size was to the dinosaur. It is a barrier to new and unvisualized directions in the natural process. Unless man retains his flexibility to readapt to nature, he will become an extinct species. With the concentration on cortical control and separation from other organic processes, man may be, without realizing it, in the twilight of his existence. Let us hope that the process of overintellectualization and static thought is reversible.

Dr. Moustakas presents a way to rediscover harmony and rhythm with nature. By concentrating on personal encounter with the immediacy of experience and using this as the focus of the learning process, the student never becomes disassociated from his own inner natural strivings. He remains authentic, makes those choices that confirm life, and evolves values that enable him to fulfill his human potentialities. This inner human formative process is a reflection of the universal process of nature. Thus, the individual maintains his connection with the natural process and can remain sensitive to new directions in universal evolution.

This book presents a way for education to help direct the learner back to life's processes. It is a timely book and is desperately needed by an educational system that is alienated from its students. I only hope it is not too late.

Eugene D. Alexander
Tri-County Guidance Center
Harrisburg, Pennsylvania

CHAPTER 1

Alienation, Education, and Existential Life

Every person is, by nature, a potentially creative being with a unique destiny and with resources for genuine encounters in the world. Yet, in spite of these capacities for individual and communal growth, men have turned away from themselves and from each other. Increasingly, men have moved toward external directions and values that will bring recognition, status, prestige, and power. Most meetings have come to be superficial, stereotyped exchanges that have little meaning or relevance either for self-development or for group life.

Modern life is not centered in genuine interhuman experience between real persons, nor does it encourage diversity and individuality. Ambitious parents set up goals and communicate expectations, either indirectly and deviously, so that what they really want and expect from the child registers clearly at subliminal levels regardless of what they say or do, or quite openly, they program the child's life in such a way that he progresses step by step toward their values, toward their goals, toward their expected achievements. Often, the individual is unaware that he, as a unique, growing person, has been canceled out and that in place of his genuine self is a concept, a definition of what should be; and that definition has been pieced together and executed in such a way that what the individual has become lacks substance and identity, which alone can give meaning to his life.

The living qualities of sensitivity and awareness remain hidden, dwarfed, and undeveloped. But the self is not its concept any more than a tree or any living thing is its definition. The parts pieced together do not make an integrated whole. They continue to exist as fragments of a self, a self that can achieve unity only through diversity of expression of real feelings and real desires and real interests, only through the expression of self-values; and these, in many important ways, will always be independent, idiosyncratic, and unusual. The mode or average (regardless of theories of numbers and mechanics) is only a statistical construct, an abstraction. It is not the living stuff, the ideal, or even the healthy path for men to take. For all its safety and comfort features, the golden mean is still only a fictitious and mechanical number. It exists as desirable in fantasy, although that fantasy may be more real for "average" persons than reality itself.

Unfortunately, the "average" does not remain in tables and charts and textbooks but finds its way into the schools and into the dead process of modern education. Here the activities are often dull, repetitive, and unimaginative. The already alienated child is grouped and lesson-planned so that he takes one more step into exile, moves further and further away from his own unique self, and, at last, becomes convinced that he is average and that his averageness is all there is to him. He rejects the one dimension of himself that can still bring meaning to his existence, his own yes-feeling, his own senses, which tell him which experiences have significance and validity. Nothing of the substance of his being, nothing of his particularity has been recognized. The values and resources that exist within the deep regions of himself have not been tapped and explored, and so he becomes one of the sea of faces, one of the modulated and patterned voices. Along with the subject matter, *he* becomes programmed and his uniqueness in the world remains unnoticed. He is anxious to please, so the indifference to his real self does not matter in the least. He got that way in the first place because he was not valued. His parents did not take their cues from him, did not love him as an independent self with his own strange and peculiar avenues of expression. They did not help him to discover new regions and to explore new territories that would get their initial value from him, from the movements of his body, from his growing awareness of life, and from his wish to explore life on his own terms. Weiss describes the destructive process as follows [14]:

> Early he begins to move away from his self, which seems not good enough to be loved. He moves away from what he is, what he feels, what he wants. If one is not loved for what one is, one can at least be safe — safe perhaps by being very good and perfect and being loved for it, or by being very strong and being admired or feared for it, or by learning not to feel, not to want, not to care. Therefore, one has to free oneself from any need for others, which means first their love and affection and, later on, in many instances, sex. Why feel, why want, if there is no response? So the person puts all his efforts into becoming what he *should* be. Later, he idealizes his self-effacement as goodness, his aggression as strength, his withdrawal as freedom. Instead of developing in the direction of increasing freedom, self-expression, and self-realization, he moves toward safety, self-elimination, and self-idealization.

Thus, the young child searching for identity and self-affirmation, lacking recognition and threatened by the withdrawal of love, launches himself into an alien life and becomes estranged from his real self. He substitutes the spontaneous, flowing self for a controlled, calculating self-system dominated by the rules and "shoulds" of the adult world. Not only does alienation set in, but there is also an absence of growing identity.

The original self-awareness becomes self-deception, and the individual no longer realizes that he has abnegated his real self in favor of a substitute.

Alienation, that is, choosing a life outlined and determined by others, rather than a life based on one's own inner experience, soon leads to desensitization. The individual stops trusting his own feelings and, since he cannot actually make another's feeling his own, he learns mechanically or automatically to make the proper gestures or facial expressions to denote the appropriate feelings; a smile is not a smile, joy is not joy, and sadness is not sadness; the movements of the face and body are properly placed to take on the appearance of the appropriate emotions. (Of course, a sensitive and perceptive person comes to know the difference between the counterfeit expression and the real thing.) The alienated person is anesthetic; he is embedded in a world without color, without excitement, without risk and danger, without mystery—in a word, without meaning. It is only one step from here to self-abnegation, when the person, without awareness, renounces himself and takes on the pattern of the authority; he conforms to the parent, the friend, the teacher, the wife or husband, the boss, the middle-class society; and he learns to play his role with increasing complexity and skill. In terms of alienation, there is not much difference between patterning and programming and being patterned and programmed. Both the programmer and the programmed are alienated in themselves and from each other.

Blindness and self-deception exist in schools where alienation is taken as a sign of healthy adjustment; where sophistication becomes a substitute for honesty, simplicity, and sincerity; where assertive individuality creates a battleground for teacher and pupil conflict; where the ones in power defeat a genuine existence through conditioning, use of external symbols of status and reward, authoritarian persuasiveness, and numerous consequences that are employed in order to crush rebellion and resistance and overwhelm and defeat the stubborn person. The child in school very soon becomes separated and detached; he becomes alienated from his work. No wonder recess becomes the most wonderful part of his day. He has no real connection to the activities that are scheduled and programmed for him. They are unrelated to him. The more he is able to keep his own private views and feelings, his own style and tempo, out of the assignments and lessons, the better his chance for achieving good results.

Desensitization occurs through a process of deprivation and separation, where one is treated as an object; where skills and subject matter are more significant than learners; where goals must be pursued regardless of the real wishes, aspirations, and capacities of persons; where rationalizing, explaining, and analyzing take the place of spontaneity, humanistic experience, and natural feeling. The adult who observes, manipulates, and directs, the adult who notes the child, probes him, writes him up, and breaks him down into specific traits of weakness and strength is actually treating the child as a thing, and the child soon learns to react like one. When the child is perceived as an object for intellectual and social nourishment, when he is treated as a member of a group or mass society, without reference to his unique and varying differences, there is real danger that he will lose touch with his own senses, with his own identity as a growing person. He will begin to build a wall around himself to protect himself against the penalties of being honest and forthright. He will become insensitive to laughter and mimicry and sarcasm, insensitive to the range of feelings that characterize genuine human existence. In short, he will become alienated from any kind of meaningful endeavor.

The student in school is alienated in the same way that any worker can become alienated from his work. The child develops an estranged attitude toward his school work; he is outside of it; he is cut off from his own self; he is alienated. School work becomes a drudge, a bore; the child engages in it only under coercion and compulsion, either from the threat of reprisal and punishment by the teacher or from the restrictive demands and directives of his "should" system. Marx, despite limitations in his views of the ideal society, had a clear vision of how meaninglessness and alienation set in when the individual does not participate as a creative self in his work. He offers an insightful description of the consequences of alienation [7]:

> . . . labour is external to the worker; i.e., it does not belong to his essential being; in his work, therefore, he does not affirm himself but denies himself, does not feel content but unhappy, does not develop freely his physical and mental energy but mortifies his body and ruins his mind. The worker, therefore, only feels himself outside his work, and in his work feels outside himself. He is at home when he is not working and when he is working he is not at home. His labour is, therefore, not voluntary, but coerced; it is *forced labour.* . . . Its alien character emerges clearly in the fact that as soon as no physical or other compulsion exists, labor is shunned like the plague. . . . the external character of labour for the worker appears in the fact that it is not his own but someone else's, that it does not belong to him, that in it he belongs, not to himself, but to another. . . . It is not spontaneous activity; it is the loss of his self.

In the same way, the child shuns school. All day long he engages in activities that are alien to him, alien to him not only as a person but also as an individual. First of all, the teacher constructs the lessons, not spontaneously and out of values and interests of a particular group, but out of a teacher's manual that dictates the number of pages that should be covered, the questions that should be asked, and the knowledge that should be gleaned. The lesson is planned not for an individual learner but for a mass society that is often divided into three classes: the fast class, the average class, and the slow class. The teacher works with group concepts and abstract goals, and the concepts and abstractions set the stage and determine the nature of the performance.

Viewing the child as a learner who is fast or slow or industrious or lazy, or in any rubrics or categories, is a way of escaping from him and avoiding the range of feelings that emerge in genuine meetings with others. Considering the child as the "other" is all part of the estrangement that results when professional and social roles separate and alienate adult and child as persons. No wonder the child feels that school is a burden and that work is a chore. No wonder there is no fun and enjoyment in learning, no real involvement. He is denied; as a self, he simply does not exist. His own feelings, perceptions, interests, senses, his own spontaneous directions are ignored. He is no longer an active force participating in the shape and destiny of his life and involved and committed so that his diversity of expression becomes indigenous to the real growth of his self. He is not free; he has no genuine choice; and he is not responsible in any meaningful sense of the term. One may observe an elementary school classroom for hours without recording one instance of individual creativity or free choice, except when the teacher's back is turned [11]. But the child's restlessness, boredom, resistance, and joy in escape are all signs that the inner self still exists, that the individual is searching for some meaningful ties to life.

The teacher who focuses on facts and knowledge, on intellectual dimensions of the self, is limiting in another respect. Not only does this attitude reinforce alienation and desensitization, but it also contributes to fragmentation. For all its significance, intelligence represents only one aspect of man, one kind of value—intellectual value. The exaggerated emphasis on intellectual accomplishment is ill advised in another sense; intelligence is not the highest level of value. In his study of values, Hartman concluded that intellectual values are the least significant in the growth of the self. These come from our systemic dimension, the dimension that builds systems, constructs rules and regulations, and stresses routine, order, duty, and discipline as maxims of life. An extreme example of how intellectual values can be used destructively and why they can never be the basis for ultimate human values and actions is contained in Hartman's analysis of Eichman [4]:

> Was Eichman a bad man? Oh, not at all. He did his duty. He said, "I never killed anybody. I am a transportation specialist. My work was to make schedules—railroad schedules. That's all I did. I followed my orders. It wasn't my business to know who was being put into these railroad cars. I never put anybody in. It wasn't my business where they went to. My orders were to make railroad schedules and that's what I did. I transported people." Well, he transported them to the fire, but that was incidental. He did it with great thoroughness and was proud of it. He was a very systematic man and the system was his life. . . . This is systemic value. It is amoral—as is the law and as is science. Both are systems. This ammorality may be immoral and it may also be moral. It all depends on how the system is being used. We can't live without systemic values—but we mustn't overdo them. All the other values are more important than systemic values, no matter how important are systemic values.

Intellectuality, convention, the system are out of focus today; they are overstressed and overused in their stranglehold on society. The system is powerfully presented in all of its devastating terror in Ken Kesey's novel of how subtle, devious brainwashing devices and indirect threats are used by intelligent, educated, professional people to subdue and defeat spontaneous human interests and impulses; eventually the "combine" (as Ken Kesey calls it) destroys individual integrity, individuality, and human decency [6]. The system is rooted in mechanics and laws which are no more, ultimately, than the values of authoritarian individuals who prefer death to life, submission to courage, routines and habits to inventiveness and ingenuity, and, on the whole, anything that will pass for order, organization, and efficiency. With its emphasis on maintaining the status hierarchies, on conducting a smooth-running operation, and on squelching deviating individuals, the system prevents the realization of higher values and experiences that are necessary for a healthy life in a healthy society.

In the classroom, the system too often determines the life that exists in the schools rather than being determined by it. The system orders the class size and sets up a curriculum and standards, requires lesson plans, defines the teacher, and assigns roles and functions. The system of administrators and supervisors and hierarchies creates a split in the lives of people. Children and teachers alike are being ruled and instructed by unseen hands and minds and often voices from faraway places, and above all by authority, the authority of the teacher who gets instruction from the principal, who gets instruction from the supervisor, who gets instruction from the assistant superintendent, who gets instruction from the superintendent. It is hardly surprising to find so much confusion, distortion, and hypocrisy in the schools and a superabundance of cliches and euphemisms. Clarity of expression, individuality, being-for-itself are rare occurrences. As Aldous Huxley has said [5]:

> To provide themselves with a recognizable identity, a niche in the scheme of things that they can call "home," they will give assent to the unlikeliest dogmas, conform to the most absurd and even harmful rules of thought, feeling and conduct, put on the most extravagant, fancy dress and identify themselves with masks that bear almost no resemblance to the faces they cover. "Bovarism" (as Jules de Gaulter calls it) is the urge to pretend that one is something that, in fact, one is not. It is an urge that manifests itself, sometimes weakly, sometimes with overpowering strength, in all human beings, and one of its manifestations is precisely our uncertainty about where we stand and who we are.

---

[1] Reprinted, by permission, from DAEDALUS, Journal of the American Academy of Arts and Sciences, Boston. Spring 1962, "Science and Technology in a Contemporary Society."

Major emphasis on intellectual programs, standards, and goals too often results in bovarism and a fraudulent life. In any case, intellectual values represent one component of the self.

The deepest level of value is self value. It is the vertical dimension within us. "The self is our reservoir of power," says Hartman. He adds [4]:

We have infinite power within us, infinitely deep down within us. It is not easy to tap this power. We can only tap it if we get rid, so to speak, of the horizontal dimension, that of society and even the little flag, on top, thinking. We are like icebergs. Most of us is underneath and the horizontal part is on top, swimming on the water like the top of an iceberg, or even better, like a water lily, very fragile. This horizontal part is our social self, the ME rather than the I. It is connected socially with other such selves—and the web of connections is called Society.

Hartman symbolizes the level of values as follows:

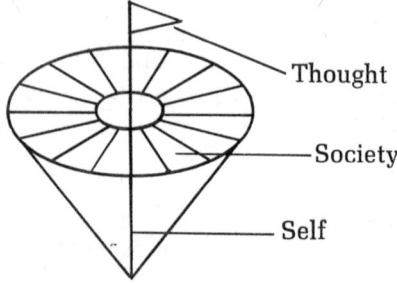

Thought

Society

Self

It is this deep level of the self, the resources and talents that exist in each of us to be formed and shaped into a particular being in the world, that the schools should recognize, encourage, and affirm. The self cannot emerge and develop unless there is freedom, choice, and responsibility, unless each person experiences himself and from the experience of his own senses becomes an active force in life, free to choose and select, free to feel and express openly and honestly the nature of these feelings, free to be responsible for the evolution of his real self, free to identify with living forces, with alive teachers who encourage growth in individual identity, who value being for itself, and who can enable the individual to engage in meaningful inquiry and activity.

Life comes from life, and the teacher is the living agent in the school. As a living agent, the teacher must not abdicate the human dimensions that he can communicate to the child: respect for his individuality;

recognition of his particular interests, needs, and directions; encouragement of his growth in identity. The human talents, the human resources of the teacher are the teacher's primary value in the educative process. Within the context of these personal, human attributes, significant and enduring learning can occur.

There is no question that teaching machines are more capable of transmitting certain facts to the pupil than the teacher, and, increasingly, ways will be found to program subject matter into lessons for more efficient and effective results. Machines are often more efficient than human beings, but efficiency and expediency are not the primary values, nor the highest values in human growth and development. Facts are insufficient as a basis for learning. They have relevance in the context of human experience. The dead facts from a dead record will not reveal the living meaning. Facts must exist in a broader realm to have integrative and unified meaning.

Self-values can never be developed by machines; they require human recognition, human nourishment, encouragement, and support, human resources, interpersonal communion and exchange, and human affirmation. Lawrence Frank has registered this warning [2]:

> If teaching is to be only the transmission of standardized knowledge, of objective facts and generalizations and the training of pupils in academic skills, then teachers will soon become obsolete, another victim of automation. But teaching, as communication by a teacher, involves not only words but also the whole range of non-verbal communication, posture, stance, the position and movements of the head, facial expressions, such as smiling, frowning, gestures of hands and arms, and varying tones of voice which color and infuse the teaching with personal significance and make lessons more than the transmission of objective materials. These non-verbal communications are like the overtones in music which give it richness, color, and, in human communications, the infinite variety of shadings and inflections, the truly individualized personal flow that evokes a meaningful response. . . . Thus, teaching is essentially a series of interpersonal relations, of human communica-

tions which are intended, not primarily to transmit content, but to evoke in the recipient pupil the responses we call learning and to give the individual pupil confidence in himself for learning to learn.

Only in this way, as a unique person with deep and varied experience, is the teacher irreplaceable. The teacher must go beyond the intellectual values that can often best be taught by impersonal, detached devices, and must immerse himself in the infinite sources of his own real self, be open to his own senses and to the particular individuals before him, both as individuals and as persons, realizing that the child's identity is being formed; his dignity and integrity are soft and vulnerable and can easily be threatened and shattered. The teacher must be present as a whole person, open to the expanding reality that every situation contains, and aware that each person is unique both in the way in which he learns and in what he learns. Being sensitive to the individual's awareness of his mode of being in the world, having a listening and perceptive attitude, and pointing to resources and opportunities that have meaning and relevance will evoke the being of the child to responsible self-actualization and to a sound and healthy identity.

Each person is centered in himself, and the roots of the self grow and flourish in meaningful experiences. The person must choose and shape these experiences for himself, because they hold for him a personal value as well as an enrichment of the world in which he lives. No teacher can be deprived of making a choice between creative spontaneous living and conformity to a system, between determining the life in the classroom and being determined by administrative dictum and policy. Even under the most authoritarian system, even with the most rigid rules and instructions, the teacher still has the freedom to choose. Viktor Frankl, in his book *From Death Camp to Existentialism* [3], wrote:

> We who lived in concentration camps can remember the men who walked through the huts comforting

others, giving away their last piece of bread. They may have been few in number, but they offer sufficient proof that everything can be taken from a man but one thing —the last of the human freedoms—to choose one's attitude in any given set of circumstances, to choose one's way.

And there were always choices to make. Every day, every hour, offered the opportunity to make a decision, a decision which determined whether you would or would not submit to those powers which threatened to rob you of your very self, your inner freedom; which determined whether or not you would become the plaything of circumstance, renouncing freedom and dignity, to become molded into the form of the typical inmate.

This same challenge, this same choice faces every teacher: to be a typical teacher, submitting to the curriculum and the prescribed rules and instructions; or to be his real self, meeting children as persons, living spontaneously, and making decisions in terms of the requirements as they emerge and unfold. It is basically a choice between conventionality and creativity, between existing in categories and playing roles and being a whole person. The making of choices is important in another sense. In the child, choices are beginning steps in the creation of values that will identify the child as a unique person; in the teacher, choices are reflections of further refinement and actualization of the self, reflections that mirror the identity of the teacher—the teacher's beliefs, convictions, preferences. By his choices, the authentic person creates himself. He chooses one thing rather than another because that choice enables him to become more fully himself. If a course of action authenticates his being, the person can believe in, gain conviction in, what the world is and who he is; then further choice and self-growth are open to him [13].

Aldous Huxley has remarked that a good education makes the best of all the worlds in which children as human beings live. He asks: "Just how good is modern education?" Here is his answer [5]:

> In science and technology specialization is unavoidable and, indeed, absolutely necessary. But training

for this unavoidable and necessary specialization does nothing to help young amphibians to make the best of their many worlds. Indeed, it pretty obviously prevents them from doing anything of the kind. . . . When courses in the humanities are used as the only antidote to too much science and technology, excessive specialization in one kind of symbolic education is being tempered by excessive specialization in another kind of symbolic education. . . . two varieties of the same world—the world of symbols. But this world of symbols is only one of the worlds in which human beings do their living and their learning. . . . education in the non-verbal humanities is not just a matter of gymnastics and football, of lessons in singing and folk-dancing. All of these, of course, are good, but by themselves not good enough. Such traditional methods of training young people in non-verbal skills need to be supplemented, if they are to yield their best results, beginning with a thorough training in elementary awareness (awareness of internal events). . . . Our amphibiousness is clearly illustrated in the two modes of our awareness of external events. There is a receptive, more or less unconceptualized, aesthetic and "spiritual" mode of perceiving; and there is also a highly conceptualized, stereotyped, utilitarian, and even scientific mode. . . . We temper a too exclusive concentration on scientific symbols . . . not with lessons in watching and receiving, but with the injunction to concentrate on philosophical and sociological symbols, to read the books that are reputed to contain a high concentration of "the spirit breathed from dead men to their kind." (Alas, dead men do not always breathe a spirit; quite often they merely emit a bad smell.)

In other words, each teacher must be fully open to the many regions of himself, to the multiple worlds in which he lives. Concentration on narrow goals, objectives, lesson plans, focus on facts and knowledge, use of authority figures, textbooks, and teachers' manuals, all contribute to external forms, to a restrictive life that is ultimately self-denying and alienating. Being open to the inherent life in the classroom means being open to one's own inner life as a person, centering oneself in evolving perceptions and being aware of transcending values and meanings in meditation, self-inquiry, and self-awareness. It also means encountering life and relating to it as an open self.

ALIENATION, EDUCATION, AND EXISTENTIAL LIFE 15

Being open in this sense enables the person to break through to meaningful self-expression (regardless of past experience) and to shine forth as an individual. Medard Boss expresses this value as follows [1]:

> This human existence consists primarily in an elucidating meaning-disclosing awareness and world openness. As such we are claimed by all the phenomena we encounter, to serve them as the necessary open and luminating realm into which they can shine forth and be the phenomena which they are, for you know the very word phenomenon is derived from the Greek word "phainestai." This simply means, "that which shines forth, and shows itself." . . . Thus, man's existence and the phenomena that present themselves into his awareness are mutually self-sustaining and but one and the same inseparable occurrence which emerges out of the mystery of concealment and no-thingness. To be this necessary world openness is exactly the nature of man.

In a climate of learning conducive to self-growth, the individuality of the learner is completely accepted and the life of the child is his own. All that a teacher can do is create a climate and offer resources and opportunities in which this life emerges, evolves, grows. In such a setting, the uniqueness of the child is valued as sheer personal being and the child is free, in the light of available materials and resources, to make choices and decisions, to determine his own direction, and to discover his own reality. Tenderness, care, and personal warmth all affect the child's experience. To recognize the otherness of the child means to respect him as a valuable being in his own autonomy and independence and to understand him in his own terms, through genuine presence and communion.

In Salinger's story "Teddy [12]," Teddy is asked, "What would you do if you could change the educational system?" He responds with these drastic recommendations:

> I know I'm pretty sure I wouldn't start with the things schools usually start with. I think I'd first just assemble all of the children and show them how to meditate. I'd

try to show them how to find out who they *are*, not just what their names are and things like that. . . . I guess, even before that, I'd get them to empty out everything their parents and everybody ever told them. I mean even if their parents just told them an elephant's big, I'd make them empty *that* out. An elephant's only big when it's next to something else—a dog or a lady, for example. . . . I wouldn't even tell them an elephant has a trunk. I might *show* them an elephant if I had one handy, but I'd let them just walk up to the elephant not knowing anything more about it than the elephant knows about them. The same thing with grass and other things. I wouldn't even tell them grass is green. Colors are only names. I mean if you tell them grass is green, it makes them start expecting the grass to look a certain way—*your* way. . . . Besides, if they wanted to learn all that other stuff—names and colors and things—they could do it, if they felt like it, later on when they were older. But I'd want them to *begin* with all the real ways of looking at things not just the way all the other apple-eaters look at things.

This vision of an existential education is expressed in several of my meetings with David [10], an unusual, creative nine-year-old who happened to be in trouble in school because he insisted on an existential life in the classroom and rejected the canned sequence and programmed lessons of his teacher, which he found empty, sterile, and meaningless. In the following comments he describes the fresh, integrative, perception of experience in contrast to the conventional perceptions that grow out of definition, repetition, and a fixation on comparisons and parts. He describes the difference between genuine encounters with life and the conformist's teachings.

David: I have lots of special feelings that there are no words for . . . not good or bad, just a full feeling— all over—and it is very comfortable. . . . If others could see inside me, they could know my feeling. There are no words to give a picture of how you feel inside. *(Pause)* Right now, as I look out the window, I don't see a road that looks like a T. That's what I've been taught is there. When I was little I didn't have to think about it. Sometimes I still don't. *(Pause)* I can be in a trance and not know what's going on around me. Someone can even ask me questions which I answer without even knowing it, when I'm open to nature. But people expect you nowadays to see things in a certain way. Sometimes you have to concentrate to see things as they really are to you. Out there, right now, I see a fuzziness in that place where the road is—its brickiness and grayness is blending with the buildings and the trees and everything outside merges, comes together, and becomes alive, all living things. . . . Look, everything so fresh and green. That's a special feeling. It sort of brings me close to everything, you know, feels sort of spiritual, everything I see. Everything seems like it's available and the way things are. . . . You might think it was something different if people didn't call it a road and say what it was for. You might see it as a pattern or a contrast to something else out there. You could put it in your own thinking and imagining. . . . If you really look, you can see a design in everything. . . . It's different from what others say are real things. It kind of takes it away when you're told it's not that way. . . . There's a particular feeling that comes along with these designs. Everything comes together. It seems like everything is available. I just look at all of it like it was together and I'm kind of glad I'm in the world, you know. That's what I mean.

The emphasis on direct, primary experience, on using one's own senses, on perceiving reality freshly and naively is necessary. Through direct encounters, the child affirms himself, enlarges his meaning in the world, and achieves a heightened sense of integration, a meeting of the center of himself with ongoing life, the wonder, excitement, and mystery of the living communion. The two aspects of encounter—*meditation, isolation, solitude, self-communion* and *communication and communion with others and with aspects of the universe*—provide the opportunity for creative realization of one's own being.

To engage in encounter one must be responsible for himself; one must be himself and affirm his individuality. Van Cleve Morris puts it this way [8]:

> He [Man] is open-ended, unspecified being. He fits in no system, no dogma, no method. For a man does

not have to be a gregarious man to be a man. He does not have to be rational, or reverent, or scientific. All he has to do is to exist, to awaken to his own existence, and then to take charge of his own life by taking ultimate responsibility for it.

Unfortunately, there is much in everyday life to interfere with authentic development of the self—the humdrum of everyday living, drifting with convention, being stuck by rules and regulations instead of openly meeting life, yielding to pressures, compromising, doing the expected, and everything that passes for morality, particularly the superficial cliches and the rules of convention and propriety. Other forces that hinder the development of the self include playing a role, doing one's duty, and the interpretation and analysis of people and events. In general, all efforts and actions directed toward looking behind reality, explaining, understanding, and justifying its existence, interfere with direct, primary, authentic experience. The authentic person, rooted in himself and not stuck in a system of fixed procedures, policies, and regulations, does not analyze and explain reality; he engages in it freely, openly, immediately, spontaneously. In this way, he achieves new integrations, new meanings, and growing actualizations of his own identity.

In relation to education, this means the teacher is in the process of becoming himself and thus, catching glimpses of life from the child, opens new pathways for learning and relatedness, new opportunities for authentic experience. Every experience that will enable the child to become himself is authentic. Becoming oneself means having freedom to choose, making decisions, and taking responsibility for one's actions. It means commitment and engagement, involvement as a self, which leads to culminating, actualizing experiences. In the authentic classroom, the concern of the teacher is not with facts or objects but with the experience undergone, with the process of becoming oneself in experience. Vandenberg describes the teacher's presence as follows [13]:

The "teacher" will not have to know what "experiences" have been undergone by the "pupil," for these would determine the immediate situation in the classroom. The authentic teacher, by refusing to objectify the pupil, is always where the pupil is, exactly and in every instance. Not to be confused with the concept of "empathy," which, from the existential viewpoint, is a form of self-induced inauthenticity (one imagines he can "feel with" the other, who is objectified in the process), nor with the prevailing concept of "acceptance" which would be to objectify the pupil and his "needs" or "interests" (with suspended judgment but still with objectification); meeting the pupil where he is consists of meeting the immediate problematic situation together in existential communication. The authentic teacher . . . is capable of responding in an immediate situation so as to become what he can become. . . . The classroom is an immediate situation of the most challenging type. Perforce, the teacher meets the pupil where he is.

For example, in presenting a poem, the teacher simply presents it—not to teach or instruct, but only because it expresses a significant dimension of the teacher's world. It has meaning and value for the teacher. As a poem, it is a real poem, a poem that fills the teacher with an aliveness and an aesthetic feeling; not merely a poem that should be included or taught, but one that compels, invites, activates the teacher, one that challenges the teacher to new awareness and meaning. The teacher does not paraphrase, explain, guide the pupils, or ask questions. All of these methods would objectify the poem. In authentic experience, the person and the environment are in collaboration, the poem is a primary source of experience and enlists or invites participation. In the process of relating and experiencing, the individual and the environment become fully integrated, and the distinction of self to universe disappears. All efforts to explain and analyze the poem objectify it in such a way that aesthetic, integrative experience is destroyed. Vandenberg remarks [13]:

> All the teacher can do is somehow or other insure relationship of the poem with life—with the pupil's own

existence. . . . Further, if all goes well it will be an experience in its own right. . . . the teacher-pupil relationship will result in an absence of objectification of each other; there will be confirmation.

In the process of presenting a meaningful resource—a reading, a play, a poem, a story—the teacher, if authentic, is presenting himself, an aspect of his world. If the presentation engenders life, it is because the teacher believes in it, is filled with it, in such a way that an integration is achieved between the teacher and the source. While presenting the source, a new experience is created, an experience that might serve both in itself, as an aesthetic moment of revelation or disclosure for the child, and at the same time as the impetus for further inquiry and self-realization. No resource will be experienced in the same way by two people; it has no exclusively objective value, but if it is real, if it is genuine, it can initiate a process of experience in the learner; the experience itself will be personal, subjective, and dependent upon the particular uniqueness of the learner.

The authentic teacher has few discipline problems [13]. Being himself is the surest way for the teacher to be respected by his students. Students are repelled by alienated teachers. If the teacher is authentic and a disciplinary situation arises, it is either because the student is not being what he can be (in other words, he does not wish to be a trouble-maker but becomes one in conflict with himself) or it is the result of his being what he chooses to be, which happens to run counter to prevailing modes of conduct (in other words, he becomes a trouble-maker). In either case, the problem can be handled as an existential confrontation. The teacher can face the issue with the student and, through struggle and compassion, come to a resolution of the problem in terms of clarification or change in behavior. In such a conflict, teacher and child remain together constructively, as real persons, and do not resort to destructive powers and tactics [9].

As it now stands, the school is a powerful reinforcer of alienation in modern society. The teacher is alienated in himself: he does not exist as a real person in the classroom; he plays a part, a role; he fulfills duties and follows instructions. The teacher is alienated from his subject matter: it is external to his real world of feelings—anger, joy, sadness, loneliness, imagination, excitement, compassion; it is outside of himself. The teacher is also alienated from the child: the child is perceived in categories and evaluative terms—as slow or fast, as an outstanding achiever or an underachiever, as average or retarded, and in many, many other traits and classifications, all of which have relevance in the object-to-object relationship but not in encounter and in self-actualization. In such a setting, where the teacher is alienated from himself, from the subject matter, and from his pupils, gradually but definitely, the teacher becomes an object among objects, a thing among things.

Authenticity and genuine self-development require the teacher's presence as a whole person, not simply a professional worker with so many degrees and a certain kind of training, but a real person with feelings, with dreams, with courage and daring, with an alive interest and commitment to creative experience for himself and for the child. Genuine life in the classroom requires that the teacher be himself and that the child be himself. The freedom of the teacher to be will encourage authentic self-expression from the child. The subject becomes a vehicle, a means of communication and relatedness; but it has meaning only when it is rendered within a human framework. When it is integrated within the teacher and infuses the teacher with deep feeling and conviction, it is authentic. Then it ceases to be a series of dead facts from a dead book and becomes part of the flow of life—raw materials in and through which the child can encounter life and derive meaning and value from his study and learning. The child is being affirmed as a genuine self, as a being in process, and through his search and inquiry he discovers new perspectives, enlarging insights, and deepened realities. The child is collaborating with life and expanding his horizons as a self. This kind of human venture, which has meaning for the growing identity of the self, can never be objective. In any venture of real significance, the individual is a lonely traveler, seeing for the first time and making discoveries with reference to his own particular self.

The objective side of subject matter is only fragments. Subject matter becomes authentic when the teacher and the child are absorbed in it, compelled by it, challenged and confronted by it as persons so that while something is taken away, something is also left behind. It is the experience itself that has meaning and value, and the quality of the experience determines the immediate challenge to current and future life. Vandenberg is emphatic in pointing out this value [13]:

> The significance is in the quality of the experience, not content; the extent to which it enables one to be open to future experience, to let one become himself, is the educative value. As the artist can take any "subject matter" and make it into a work of art, which by the principle of continuity is only saying that he can take any experience and render it communicable, so too can the teacher use any experience. He merely needs to be open to it. . . . As the artist is open to his immediate situation and uses it to create a work of art that is his communication, so, too, is the teacher open to the immediate situation of the classroom.

What are the conditions that facilitate freedom, choice, and responsibility, the conditions that encourage authentic existence in the classroom? Rogers has abstracted these conditions from the pioneering efforts of creative educators and from pertinent research in psychotherapy and in the classroom. It is necessary that the individual, at whatever level of education, be confronted by resources, issues, and problems that are meaningful and relevant to him. It is essential that the teacher hold an unyielding and deep trust in the child as a person of value, with capacities and talents that, when free to be expressed, will eventuate in positive and constructive experiences. If we trust the capacity of the individual for developing his own potentiality, we can permit him the opportunity to choose his own way in his learning. It is important that the teacher be a real person—enthusiastic, sad, angry, joyful, calm, excited—that he stand out in an honest way with the range of feelings that differentiate the living person from the mechanical role-player. It is essential that the teacher prize the child as a person, be aware of and value his feelings and thoughts, convey genuine understanding based on the child's own perceptions, and accept his tempo and pace, his way of perceiving and relating to the life of the classroom. It is also important that the teacher provide resources. Rogers explains this condition as follows:

> Instead of organizing lesson plans and lectures, such a teacher concentrates on providing all kinds of relevant raw material for use by the students, together with clearly indicated channels by which the student can avail himself of these resources. I am thinking not only of the usual academic resources—books, workspace, tools, maps, movies, recordings, and the like. I am also thinking of human resources, persons who might contribute to the knowledge of the student. Most important in this respect is the teacher himself as a resource. He makes himself and his special knowledge and experience clearly available to the students, but he does not impose himself on them. He outlines the particular ways in which he feels he is most competent, and they can call on him for anything he is able to give, but this is an offer of himself as a resource, and the degree to which he is used is up to the students. . . . He does not assign readings. He does not lecture or expound (unless requested to). He does not evaluate and criticize unless the student wishes his judgment on a product. He does not give examinations. He does not set grades. . . . He is actually, operationally, giving his students the opportunity to learn to be responsibly free.

Certain other principles will help to create a climate conducive to responsible self-growth:

1. The individual knows himself better than anyone else; only he lives with himself twenty-four hours of every day.

2. The individual's perceptions and expressions of his

own feelings, thoughts, and experiences are a more valid avenue of relatedness to him than any diagnosis or evaluation.

3. Only the person himself can develop his potentialities, no matter how fervently and exhaustively another person may wish to do this for him.

4. The individual, to keep on growing as a self, must continue to believe in himself, regardless of what anyone else may think about him. The belief in a reality is a primary factor in the fulfillment of that reality.

5. Objects have no meaning in themselves. Individuals ascribe meanings to them, meanings that reflect a unique background of experience.

6. Every person is logical in the context of his own personal experience and the values he has created out of these experiences. He may seem illogical to others when he is not understood in his own world of thought and feeling.

7. When the teacher accepts and values the child as a whole person, the child will perceive this as an affirmation of him and will use his energies in exploring and actualizing himself; when he is rejected and forced into a meaningless existence, he will use his resources in maintaining and defending himself, even if that self is alienated.

8. Growth of the self does not require calculated and planned external motivation from the teacher. These growth strivings are present at all times and constitute the one central tendency in each man.

9. Under externally induced threat, the basic striving for self-actualization is impaired; the self is passive, controlled, and inauthentic. Freedom from externally imposed threat, freedom to be (which may itself involve pain and frustration), enables the self to be open to life and to strive toward actualization.

10. The educational situation that most effectively promotes significant learning is one in which (a) the external threats to the self of the learner, such as rejection, criticism, evaluation, reward, and punishment, are at a minimum, while, at the same time, the individuality

and uniqueness of the person are valued, respected, and trusted; and (b) the person is free to explore the materials and resources that are available to him in the light of his own interests, potentialities, and readiness.

In such a setting, the student initially may experience much frustration, struggle, and disturbance; but gradually he comes to be responsible, creative, and free. He comes to be clearly present as a unique individual, as someone who can be known as a genuine and integrated being.

The moment for initiating an authentic life and departing from alienation and dehumanization is always present. No matter how entrenched a person is in the world of the other, in rationalizing, in analyzing, in intellectualizing, no matter how immersed the individual is in standards and values and goals of the system, he still can decide, in the next moment, to alter the course of his existence. He still can become the one he really is, create meanings and values and actualize potentialities that are consistent with his real self. No one can take this away. And for any particular person, no one can predict what the individual will do. Regardless of his past, in any situation he can choose to activate genuine talents and resources, real directions of the self. He can choose to become himself, which is the only way to authentic existence. Frankl came to this conclusion after being part of the horror and shame of four concentration camps [3]:

> Thus, every human being has the chance of changing at any instant. There is the freedom to change, in principle, and no one should be denied the use of it. Therefore, we can never predict a human being's future except within the large frame of a statistical survey referring to a whole group. On the contrary, an individual personality is essentially unpredictable. The basis for any predictions would be represented by biological, psychological, or sociological influences. However, one of the main features of human existence is the capacity to emerge from and rise above all such conditions—to transcend them. By the same token, man is ultimately transcending himself. The human person then transcends himself insofar as he reshapes his own character.

For each person the beginning is now, the present The individual can decide, whatever the turmoil of the past or the apparently fixed goals of the future, that this moment exists in its own right and can be entered into by a light from within, which leads to a genuine path of creation and meaning.

REFERENCES

1. Boss, Medard. "What Makes Us Behave At All Socially?" *Rev. of Exist. Psychol. and Psychiat.,* IV (Winter, 1964), No. 1, 53–68.
2. Frank, Lawrence K. "The Teacher As Communicator," *Wheelock Alumnae Quarterly,* XXXIV (Fall, 1963).
3. Frankl, Viktor E. *From Death Camp to Existentialism.* Boston: Beacon Press, 1960.
4. Hartman, Robert S. *The Individual in Management.* Lecture presented to The Nationwide Management Center, Columbus, Ohio, November 7, 1962.
5. Huxley, Aldous. "Education on the Non-verbal Level," *Daedalus,* XCI (Spring, 1962), No. 2, 279–293.
6. Kesey, Ken. *One Flew over the Cuckoo's Nest.* New York: Viking Press, 1962.
7. Marx, Karl, and Engels, Friedrich. "On Alienation." In C. Wright Mills (ed.), *Images of Man.* New York: George Braziller, Inc., 1960.
8. Morris, Van Cleve. "John Dewey and The Existentialist Frontier." Dewey Centennial Lecture, Rutgers University, New Brunswick, New Jersey, July 29, 1959.
9. Moustakas, Clark. "Confrontation and Encounter," *J. Of Existential Psychiatry,* II (Winter, 1962), No. 7, 263–290.
10. Moustakas, Clark. *Psychotherapy with Children: The Living Relationship.* New York: Harper and Brothers, 1959.
11. Rogers, Carl. "Learning to Be Free," (Parts I and II) *Pastoral Psychology,* XIII, No. 128, 47–54, and XIII, No. 129, 43–51.
12. Salinger, J. D. *Nine Stories.* Boston: Little, Brown and Co., 1953
13. Vandenberg, Donald. Experimentalism in the Anesthetic Society. *Harvard Educational Review,* Vol. 32, No. 2, Spring 1962, 155–187.
14. Weiss, Frederick A. Self-alienation: Dynamics and Therapy. *American J. of Psychoanalysis,* Vol. 21, No. 2, 1961, 207–218.

CHAPTER 2

Creativity and Conformity in Education

War, overpopulation, starvation, and disease are problems easily recognized as severe threats to man's continued survival and destiny. Not so clearly visible, but equally widespread, are the destructive and evil consequences of self-denial and alienation. The search for truth, meaning, and honesty, the search for authentic life, the hunger for love and communion with others, the struggle for a genuine existence based on real capacities and real talents of real persons—these are not just emotional phrases, but signs of disturbance, restlessness, and boredom in everyday life. The deterioration of meaning, the breakdown of values, the increasing substitution of machine for man, of program for person, of mass for individual, of modeling and copying for inventing and creating—all of these threaten the potential richness and beauty of human experience. The deterioration of human values faces each of us in many, many situations. There are those who understand and know but pretend not to see, and those who look on as if violence and betrayal were happening only to others; some no longer know and no longer care. If we do not see the superficial and dishonest and false in a tangible way, they do not exist. If the destructive does not impinge directly upon us, we can ignore it. For those too burdened already and too removed from hope and courage, life is static and fixed; excitement, vitality, and enthusiasm are gone. For others, it is a matter of calculated planning and managing, modulated gestures and voices, and steady gains in status, prestige, and power; a matter of building better machines and models and performing more precisely defined roles and functions.

The deterioration of human values and the betrayal of one's self are prevailing characteristics of the individual in modern society. Where freedom and choice have been denied, the individual soon comes to reject his own senses; he looks outside for a verdict on what he should be thinking and feeling and deciding. The alienated person does not make full use of his perceptions and faculties in determining which experiences contribute to self-realization and which are irrelevant or impeding; he no longer uses his own organs and powers to create reality and to venture into new life. Since the individual does not trust his own immediate experience and the response of his senses to lead him to new experience, he is neither open to himself nor to the world.

Alienation, which often begins in the home, is further intensified, extended, and reinforced in the school, where the focus is on group standards and group norms, grades, adjustment, and security. Kneller [7] describes the consequences of treating the individual as a member of a mass society:

> In order to get along, he learns to do what his teachers ask of him and what his peers expect of him. This is not faith in the self, but self-surrender. . . . to have faith in himself, the student must be able to trust his own experience of life, or, if you will, his own verdict on that experience. To this end he must be able freely to respond to life and freely to reflect on his responses.
>
> Does the school allow him this freedom? Hardly! The school screens his experience, determines what aspects of the world he will respond to, and preconsiders how he will behave in regard to them. As a result, the pupil comes to distrust his own response to

life and embraces instead the habits conditioned in him by his school.

The shrewd child picks up the appropriate form and begins to ask questions and seek explanations, without any real interest, relationship, involvement, or background. This kind of response is often given status because it flatters the teacher, who becomes an expert in the classroom and the center of attention and adulation. Profound involvement in an area of knowledge, insight, and discovery do not come by seeking or getting explanations. Genuine learning requires a sense of mutuality, an immersion into the subject—labor, exertion, and hours of searching and struggling. And the deeper the perplexity, the more burning the curiosity, the less will children seek explanations. When the learner has exhausted his study from his own searching, when he comes to the end of his own resources, if his search is authentic and self-inspired, only then does he seek additional clarification and help. The creative teacher does not explain, but turns the learner back to his own resources or helps him to acquire new ones [6].

The conforming teacher submits to the system and resorts to methods of manipulation and control. One of the most effective ways to subdue the child is to classify him. In the conventional school he is labeled—gifted, average, retarded; and he is classified—fast, average, slow. In many ways he is stereotyped and fixed and expected to play the role defined by professional nomenclature, abstract goals, and unseen faces. He is expected to become a replica of the stereotype and give up his own fresh, spontaneous contact and response to life. He is prodded; he is motivated; he is directed; he is rewarded and he is punished. He is assigned lessons from a teacher's manual, which dictates what he should read, how much, and in what manner. He moves from one subject to another by virtue of invisible authorities whom he does not know, would not recognize, and does not ever meet. His education is detached, impersonal, fragmentary, and guided by anonymous hands. No wonder school is a burden and work is a chore. No wonder, more and more, he becomes numb and deadened in the process of moving from grade to grade. No wonder there is no excitement or joy in learning and no involvement. He is denied as a self; he does not exist except as the generalized other; his creative energy is restrained, stifled, and almost totally ignored.

The school system that establishes an impersonal structure and rules and regulations to dictate appropriate behavior cuts children off from their own spontaneous awakening, from their own response to life. Kneller [7] has described the deadening impact of hierarchy and organization on creative energy:

> In the schools this energy is frustrated by regulations designed to keep masses of young people in order by making them behave in unison. It is frustrated, too, by tired, overworked teachers, who cannot spare the time to nurture the creativity of the individual student because they must struggle amid the impersonal web of administrative detail and mass guidance and counseling procedures to instill into their swollen classes the basic requirements of a stereotyped syllabus.

And what is the ultimate result—uniformity of behavior, uniformity of expression, death of individuality, docility, passivity, and conformity. In spite of the eventual capitulation to the system, there are still signs of restlessness, resistance, boredom, and chaos and disorder; when the teacher's back is turned, there are still signs that the individual is dissatisfied, that he is searching and striving to discover more meaningful avenues of expression and ties to life.

The teacher hangs on—to what?—to intellectual values, to scores, to achievements, to whatever facts can be mustered to justify the curriculum and prove that, in the end, the battle to defeat individuality, freedom, and imagination is worth the cost; in the end, the scores are higher, and the number of months of upgrading in the subject areas can be pointed to with pride. What has happened in the process? First, the child is further alienated from himself. The activities he engages in have nothing to do with his own integrity, with his own response to life. He is also alienated from his teacher, who does not exist as a person and does not recognize his uniqueness, his perceptions of reality, his commitments to life. His own feelings become blunted; his wishes are cut off and rejected as a basis for learning; his sensitivity and awareness are defeated through criticism, through external standards of conformity, and through modes of group life. Finally, the child becomes fragmented in the labels and classifications applied to him. Facts, knowledge, intellectual gains are the important values—in spite of the fact that intellectual values represent only a fragment of human life, only one dimension of existence. Thus, many of today's classrooms still carry the banner of M'Choakumchild's Schoolroom [1]:

> "Now, what I want is, Facts. Teach these boys and girls nothing but Facts. Facts alone are wanted in life. Plant nothing else, and root out everything else. You can only form the minds of reasoning animals upon Facts: nothing else will ever be of any service to them. This is the principle on which I bring up my own children, and this is the principle on which I bring up these children. Stick to Facts, sir!" . . .
> "Girl number twenty," said Gradgrind, squarely pointing with his square forefinger, "I don't know that girl. Who is that girl?"
> "Sissy Jupe, sir," explained number twenty, blushing, standing up, and curtseying.
> "Sissy is not a name," said Mr. Gradgrind. "Don't call yourself Sissy. Call yourself Cecilia."
> "It's father as calls me Sissy, sir," returned the young girl in a trembling voice, and with another curtsey.
> "Then he has no business to do it," said Mr. Gradgrind. "Tell him he mustn't. Cecilia Jupe. Let me see. What is your father?"
> "He belongs to the horse-riding, if you please, sir." Mr. Gradgrind frowned, and waved off the objectionable calling with his hand.
> "We don't want to know anything about that, here. You mustn't tell us about that, here. Your father breaks horses, don't he?"
> "If you please, sir, when they can get any to break, they do break horses in the ring, sir."
> "You mustn't tell us about the ring, here. Very well,

then. Describe your father as a horsebreaker. He doctors sick horses, I dare say?"

"Oh yes, sir."

"Very well, then. He is a veterinary surgeon, a farrier, and horsebreaker. Give me your definition of a horse."

(Sissy Jupe thrown into the greatest alarm by this demand.)

"Girl number twenty unable to define a horse!" said Mr. Gradgrind, for the general behoof of all the little pitchers. "Girl number twenty possessed of no facts, in reference to one of the commonest of animals! Some boy's definition of a horse. Bitzer, yours." . . . "Your definition of a horse."

"Quadruped. Graminivorous. Forty teeth, namely twenty-four grinders, four eye-teeth, and twelve incisors. Sheds coat in the spring; in marshy countries, sheds hoofs, too. Hoofs hard, but requiring to be shod with iron. Age known by marks in mouth." Thus (and much more) Bitzer.

"Now girl number twenty," said Mr. Gradgrind. "You know what a horse is."

---

[1] Reprinted, with permission, from *Issues in Education*, Bernard Johnston (ed.). Boston: Houghton Mifflin Company, 1964.

When intelligence is used to establish rigid systems and hierarchies, when it becomes a substitute for human concern and human involvement, then it is being used destructively, and it violates individual integrity and human decency.

The values and resources of each individual self, the potentialities and talents ready to be formed and shaped, should be recognized, encouraged, and affirmed in our schools. The human talents, the human resources of the teacher are the teacher's primary value in the educative process. As a unique individual, the teacher can be open to new experience, open to emerging life.

Being open to the inherent life in the classroom means first of all being open to one's own inner life as a person; it means centering oneself in evolving perceptions and potentialities that come to fulfillment in living itself; it means being aware of human values as well as intellectual and social values; it means being open to the unfolding process in learning and to values and meanings that include but transcend facts or techniques; it means letting each person be himself, encouraging and valuing individuality and letting it shine forth. It means recognizing the child as a valuable being in his own autonomy and independence and understanding the child through listening, communion, and genuine presence. It means being open to and participating in each experience as a new venture. It means respecting and affirming the validity of the child's perceptions and accepting as fact the reality of those perceptions for the child.

In the classroom, there are infinite possibilities for life, many directions of choice and self-actualization. Given a chance, content will emerge as the individual engages in meaningful study and work. Then knowledge becomes integral to the individual and is absorbed into the self. It is important to remember: There is no single way but many paths to depth in learning and multiple areas of knowledge and experience. All of life is a potential avenue of discovery and insight. Somehow we have lost touch with the reality of the learner as a person of infinite possibilities for encounter with many, many dimensions of life. The curriculum has been constructed to give single lessons, with single questions and single answers, rather than for diversity, variety, and multiplicity.

Genuine relationship between learner and subject takes the form of pattern rather than stimulus-response connections. Even machines are now built to recognize this fact. David Hawkins [6] makes the point clearly and strongly:

> From what we now know of informational processes, even machines designed for pattern recognition and classification will function most efficiently—when dealing with a very complex system of data—if they are deliberately programmed for such "non-directive," in some respects even random, "Monte Carlo" exploratory behavior. In spite of the anxieties about machines in our culture, it may be that the machine designers are closer to an appreciation of what is involved in human

learning than are those circumscribed by the simplistic traditions of behavioristic psychology and "programmed learning."

In an authentic education, the emphasis is on direct, primary experience, using one's own senses, perceiving reality freshly and naively, and spontaneously encountering life. In genuine encounters, the child enlarges his awareness of reality; he achieves a heightened sense of integration, a meeting of the center of himself with ongoing life, with wonder, excitement, and mystery. Through openness, whether in self-dialogue or in communication with others, creative life emerges. One way in which this openness of being can be awakened is for the teacher to encourage the child to attune himself to the intuition of his senses. Kneller [7] suggests the following:

> On his way home, should he catch sight of a flock of birds gathering against a darkening sky or a burst of sunlight flaring upon a garden wall, or should he hear the cry of traffic swept far off on the evening air, he would take these impressions to his heart and let them instruct him in their obscure and tongueless way of the mystery of things. Life itself, vaster than our expression of it, speaks to us in countless ways—in the words of a friend, in the movement of a symphony, in a breath of wind across a bed of flowers, in the sight of cities, in the sirens of factories, in the murmur of pain, in the shouts of ecstacy. If our students are to be creative, let them *listen* to life.

Of course, listening can be part of a process of dialogue, one aspect of self-expression. New creations are formed in the process of creating; conversations unfold in new directions rather than repeating old thoughts; paintings take on unexpected qualities as the painter and the paints are encountered in the fullness of being; a poem *becomes*, even while it is being written. Any expression created in the process of ongoing life may also be a step to new creation. Here are some samples of painting with words that are an outgrowth of authentic life with fifth graders [4].

Cool morning . . . dawn breaks.
The wind whispers through the trees.
Sunshine warms the earth.
                    Robin Rosenberg

Black is the night without moon or stars.
Black is the fuel coming out of a huge rocket,
A small black cat, a man's top hat.

Black is the coal you put in ships,
The watery, slimy, ugliness of oil,
The lining for a beautiful picture of colors,
Or the fall of a shadow on flowers.
                    Donald Abrahm

The glow of dawn which is so bright,
A daisy shedding its petals white,
The gulls that fly in the warm twilight,
A furry cat that creeps at night,
The taste of spring that is so light.
Do you know why "pure" is white?
                    Susan Helms

Brown is a beautiful color.
It's the color of chocolate cake,
A baseball mitt, a shadow on a lake.

Brown is the color that makes you feel proud,
Also a wheat field that's just been plowed,
The color of rooftops high in the sky
And graceful birds that soar and fly,
The posts that hold up my bed,
And the hair on the top of my head.
The brown of a person who's been in the sun,
The feeling of a child who's having fun.
A beautiful color is brown.
                    Stefanie Felix

Silence is a stream flowing to the sea,
A bee gathering pollen from the flowers,
Lying in a green carpet of grass;
Watching the clouds drift through the sky,
The lovely fragrance of flowers.
                    Susan Goodwin

In authentic experience, the subject matter is related to the learner. It arouses and sustains his interest. It is not something out there to be memorized and repeated, but rather it is raw material in the form of books, maps, movies, instruments, sounds, colors, shapes, forms, water, earth, sky, people, trees, motions, mechanics, air—dimensions of life that captivate the individual and sustain meaning and value. Any subject matter or environmental resource that extends knowledge, deepens appreciation and understanding, and expands the awareness of the learner is an appropriate source of enrichment and discovery. Hawkins' description of the curriculum of the creative kindergarten of the "progressive education" era is indicative of the kind of subject matter and life that can be engendered in the modern school [6].

> Here there was not only a style of teaching that involved children deeply in subject matter, but the subject matter grew with the style—water, sand, clay, paint, good infant literature, the cultivation of story and song, carpentry, lenses, prisms, magnets, blocks, the house of packing boxes and orange crates, soil and seed, animals, the dance, and all the rest. I do not believe that this tradition failed at all; its influence has been reduced by erosion (sometimes to the vanishing point), by pressures for thin mechanical programs of "reading readiness," "number experience," and the like, most of which tend to reduce the very readiness they seek to cultivate.

In the creative setting, initially the student may experience much frustration, struggle, and disturbance; but gradually he comes to be responsible, creative, and free. He comes to be clearly present as a unique individual, as a genuine and integrated being, as someone who can relate and grow in his life with others.

REFERENCES

1. Dickens, Charles. "M'Choakumchild's Schoolroom," in Bernard Johnston (ed.), *Issues in Education*. Boston: Houghton Mifflin Co., 1964.
2. Frank, Lawrence K. "The Teacher As Communicator," *Wheelock Alumnae Quarterly*, XXXIV (Fall 1963).

3. Frankl, Viktor E. *From Death Camp to Existentialism.* Boston: Beacon Press, 1960.
4. Goody, Marjorie. "Painting with Words." Unpublished poems, Fifth Grade, Alamo School, San Francisco, California.
5. Hartman, Robert S. *The Individual in Management.* Lecture presented to The Nationwide Management Center, Columbus, Ohio, November 7, 1962.
6. Hawkins, David. "The Informed Vision: An Essay on Science Education," *Daedalus,* XCIV (Summer 1965), 538–552.
7. Kneller, George F. *The Art and Science of Creativity.* New York: Holt, Rinehart, and Winston, Inc., 1965.
8. Moustakas, Clark. *The Authentic Teacher: Sensitivity and Awareness in the Classroom.* Cambridge, Mass.: Howard A. Doyle Publishing Co., 1966.
9. Moustakas, Clark. "Confrontation and Encounter." In *Creativity and Conformity.* Princeton, N.J.: D. Van Nostrand Co., 1967.

CHAPTER 3

The Authentic Self: The Readiness to Be

I am interested in readiness, not as an abstraction, but in the readiness of real people and in the meanings and values that underlie it. I am concerned with the particular human being—a man, a woman, a child, each with his own feelings, convictions, interests, hopes, and dreams, each with his own unique reality and his own unique destiny, a destiny that can be a continual awakening to life or a daily trial of deadening activity. To be this reality, to be this unique individual—openly, honestly, clearly—is the challenge of each person. Nowhere in today's world is basic self-honesty more threatened and more violated than in the modern school, where external authorities and status symbols are still the primary fixations.

Not to be an authentic human being—not to feel, perceive, think directly through one's own senses, and stand by one's own convictions—means to fail to meet life fully, intensely, seriously, with all the daring, risk, and imagination that true experiences engender. Readiness is simply this: the commitment, involvement, and presence of real persons, facing real problems and living through the pain and the joy of real learning. Readiness means meeting life as it emerges in all its ranges of depth and intensity. It is not some abstract capacity that suddenly appears as motivation for learning and achievement. It is not a justification for a calculated, timed assault upon a child. Rather, it is the willingness of the person to immerse himself in experience, to steep himself in the world, and to let unknown directions emerge. It is a time to savor, enjoy, digest, relate, and discover. It is the freedom to let go and enter timelessly into an unpredictable journey with other human beings; it involves all the senses and capacities, not merely the intellect. Readiness means being wide open, seeing the world as it exists; seeing each person—child, teacher, parent—as a human being (with strengths and frailties and peculiar ways), listening and feeling with the individual as he emerges as a particular self. It means enabling the person to become increasingly what he can be, maintaining human contact with this person and developing a sense of trust, self-regard, and personal integrity. The human being is not an object out there to be manipulated and molded into a false creature; rather, each is the one he actually is and no other, searching for ways to express himself and develop his potentialities. We can assist in the creative development of others by recognizing each person as a unique being of unqualified value.

In the process of coming to know a child as an individual and letting him know he is valued in his own right without reference to what he may achieve, the adult sees what interests, provokes, compels, attracts, and challenges him. The adult learns what resources and materials will validate and authenticate the learner and makes these available to him. The adult enters into dialogue with the child, shares his excitement and involvement in learning, and confirms him as being this particular individual. Thus, what the child learns is always connected to his self, to the personal world in which he lives, and to the powers and forces of life existing within him.

Unfortunately, these are not central values in the schools as I observe them today. Too often the adult is not really there as a human being or as an individual, nor is he aware and responsive to the young persons before him. Rather, he is caught in a system of external and extraneous purposes and goals, a system of authorities, and a canned curriculum that defines appropriate behavior and signs of success and failure; he is being guided by experts and authorities who often remain anonymous and invisible. When the learner bumps up against rules and regulations that interfere with his development and block his growth rather than eliminating the rule and dispensing with the system, too often it is the child who is dispensed with; it is the child who must suffer; it is the child who is belittled and shamed and inevitably frightened and defeated. And then, after being killed as a self, he pays a double penalty and is told that the rule exists for his own protection, for his own "good." As long as he resists and rebels, he has a chance to maintain his integrity, but when he sins against his own senses and comes to believe that what he actually perceives is false and what he does not experience is real, he has committed a double crime, against himself and against his belief in himself; this is what makes his life a tragedy. He is being affected by subtle, devious brainwashing methods, often in the guise of benevolence and love; he is being manipulated, but in such a way that he does not know whom he should confront or encounter; he does not know with whom he is in conflict, who is his enemy. Thus, a serious violation of his own self has occurred, an essential interference and breakdown in his own resources for personal growth. Increasingly, such a person falls short of what he could have been if he had developed in an unimpeded way, consistent with his own biological makeup. He loses touch with his own personal possibilities and his world is narrowed and constricted. Although his capacities have been inhibited, the person cannot get rid of himself or of the agony of his failure to be. Maslow [1] cites the neurotic consequences and considers them a dominant form of neurosis:

> I think for instance of the fine pianist who couldn't play before an audience of more than a few, or the phobic who is forced to avoid heights or crowds. The

person who can't study, or who can't sleep, or who can't eat many foods has been diminished as surely as the one who has been blinded. The cognitive losses, the lost pleasures, joys, and ecstasies, the loss of competence, the inability to relax, the weakening of will, the fear of responsibility—all are diminutions of humanness.

There is much in the school that contributes to this process. Too often the adult sees the young child as an unfinished creature, as an object of learning to be molded, shaped, prodded, pushed, rewarded, and reinforced. The notion that there is real value in structuring fragments of behavior and in reinforcing little facts and pieces of information and repeating these segments until they are learned is one of the most ridiculous fixations of modern educators; the notion that children learn without personal involvement and meaning is one of the greatest hoaxes of the modern school. Going through the motions of learning and learning itself are two basically different processes. Significant learning always involves the learner as a person; thus, education itself must be humanized, must include the perceptions and interests of the learner if it is to have genuine meaning.

Too often, rather than having encounters with children, rather than remaining alive and responsive, the adult observes, manipulates, and directs the child, treats him as an object for learning, as a thing, and he soon learns to react like one. When the child is perceived as an empty vessel to be filled with facts and explanations, there is real danger that he will lose touch with his own awareness and response to life. There is real danger that he will begin to build alienating defenses to protect himself against the penalties of being honest and forthright. In such a setting, learning is divorced from human values; the people in the school are alienated from each other and from themselves. The child engages in activities that have nothing to do with his own integrity, with his own response to life. He is alienated from his teacher, who does not exist as a person, who does not recognize his uniqueness, and who does not know that reality is based on personal perceptions and commitments to life, not on external purpose, motive, goal, and authority [2].

In his encounters with life, the child can enlarge his awareness of reality in a climate in which he is recognized as an individual and in which he is encouraged to develop more and more of himself. In such an atmosphere, the child achieves a heightened sense of integration; he is connected with his experience; his learning is vital, human, alive, interesting; more and more he is actualizing his creative potential, because he is involved and his involvement makes the difference between being real and playing a role, between being deceptive (and going through the motions of accomplishment to satisfy the adult) and being himself. When the self of the person is present, the person is willing to trust intuition, spontaneity, and vital forces within himself; then there is a meeting of the person with ongoing life, with wonder, excitement, mystery; the individual is carried away with the ecstasy of learning, the joy of discovery, and the meaning of new awareness. Feelings of love, imagination, and inspiration make the whole process of learning a true passion for discovery, a true awakening, a breaking through of the monotony of school life and all the dead words that pass between people and are constantly repeated among them without meaning. Learning that is real inevitably involves a struggle with life, self-involvement and exertion that deepen awareness and knowledge. The monotonous existence of repetition, reward, and reinforcement does not bring life; it merely transmits bad faith, and under the guise of scientific proof of achievement it destroys uniqueness, individuality, and personal integrity. It also destroys any sense of community, because it promotes sameness, uniformity, and a closed system of group interaction guided by rules and regulations, rather than the real limits of one's own capacities and abilities.

Instead of reinforcing preconceived notions of desirable behavior and preconceived notions of what should be learned, the adult can set his sights and senses on himself and on the learner as real persons and can enter into genuine dialogue. This means that the teacher is open to new experience and, being open, encourages the child to be in touch with his own senses—the breathing of the leaves, the feelings of his own footsteps, the movement of the clouds, the rhythm of his body in motion, the pain and suffering of his neighbor, the joy and wonder of discovery, the feel of texture and color, the meaning of laughing and crying, the beauty and excitement of a new idea. Life speaks to us in countless ways—in the words of a real friend, in the pain of defeat and accident, in the vibrations of music, in the tensions and frustrations of involvement with reality, in the feel of color and sound, in the agony of conflict and of love, in the excitement of play.

In human education, the subject matter is related to the learner and stems from his innovations, his interests, his commitments. Genuine education is not something out there—existing in fragments and pieces; rather, it is within the person's own capacities, talents, and preferences. It is within the center of the self meeting the world, and these meetings inspire, motivate, involve, enable, and encourage the person to search, inquire, and deepen his knowledge and interest. Genuine resources for learning are not objects in the minds of adults to be used to badger, motivate, compel, force, and vanquish the learner either through the manipulation of reward and punishment or the manipulation of "love" and power. Genuine learning always involves dialogue and encounter. It is not something outside to be memorized and repeated; rather, it is raw material. When it is truly relevant to a learner, a book is not merely a book but a source of encounter and relatedness, a media of interest and meaning, a source of life. Any dimension of the world that captivates the individual, sustains him as a human being, and enables him to grow is a valid source of learning. Any subject matter or environmental resource that extends knowledge, deepens appreciation and understanding, and expands the awareness of the learner is an appropriate source of enrichment and discovery. Each person is capable of wide ranges of experience that serve to open and awaken him to new avenues of expression and to new direction. Then life really moves the person. New powers, new surges of feeling are created—imminently, immediately, intensely, vividly; the person responds, talks back, engages in strange, unique dialogue, reaches out to touch life, and actualizes his potential in color (with vast variations in sensation, hue, brightness, composition), in sound (with inexpressible, utterly new vibrations and tones), in texture and touch (infinite feelings to rove over and through, encounters in unknown regions), in ideas (sailing freely in and out of the mind, new styles of thought and expression), in taste (aesthetic moments and senses coming alive in awareness, eager, avid, vital); the person reaches out to meet other human beings with a clarity and fullness of presence and, at times, in the extremes of being and feeling.

As I see it, the adult initially brings to the life of a child those resources and materials that have grown out of his own direct experiences. These are but the beginning, however—ways that the adult introduces himself to the young child, ways of saying: "Here I am and here with me are some of the resources I have found of value. You may find these materials significant, test them, explore them, use them, share them, work with them—alone, with others—use them to pursue your interests in science, literature, music, art, dance. I wish to listen, to speak, to relate, to know, to encourage, to enable you to grow more and more fully, to assist you in developing your talents and resources, and to find genuine life here for myself."

Learning must have personal meaning as facts are absorbed, as knowledge is deepened, as decisions and choices are made. New resources and materials are added as the interests and abilities of each learner unfold and develop, as the learner becomes involved in his own inquiry, as he shares himself with others. Forward movement, direction, occurs through acceptance of the learner and respect for his way and timing in learning. When, however, the learner is stuck and is becoming stagnant, the adult provokes, challenges, searches for the deeper, underlying interest and attempts to reveal this to the learner—even when it leads to resistance, resentment, and temporary breakdown in the relationship. Both acceptance and challenge have a place: the one process recognizes and encourages immediate expressions of the self; the other recognizes and encourages new involvement and commitment. A third form of meeting between adult and child involves a response to the person as if he were that which he can become; that is, believing deeply in him, in a potential reality, and thus helping it to become actualized.

The real world of the child is a world of personal meaning and involvement, a world centered in the self, with individual and peculiar forms of interests and activities. Although it is important to meet such a child intellectually and cognitively, it is much more important, for both the child and the adult, to humanize the education of the learner; to be aware of the many worlds in which people live, verbal and nonverbal, feeling, thought, spirit, aesthetic, and scientific; to keep open the doors of communication and of human relations. It is more important to keep values in the forefront in learning. In no way should human values be neglected —sensitivity, awareness, uniqueness, responsiveness, respect for the integrity of the learner and his preferences and interest, authenticity, honesty, truth, love— each has its place in everyday meetings, and each is more important than the most important fact or skill. In no way should expediency, efficiency, organization, and achievement push the self of the learner away, for the self of the learner is his one unique contribution to humanity, his one tie to meaning and to life, his one tie to responsiveness and to responsibility. To let this inner light be dimmed is to destroy a unique truth, which alone can create the lust for learning that carries the learner forward, beyond the region of the dull and commonplace and into the ingenious and the creative, beyond the narrow confines of the intellect and into the world of the senses, beyond security and status and into the responsiveness of communal living and loneliness, with all the pain and joy of human existence.

REFERENCES

1. Maslow, Abraham H. "Neurosis As a Failure of Personal Growth." Lecture presented as an Institute of Man Symposium, Duquesne University, November 18, 1966.
2. Moustakas, Clark. *The Authentic Teacher: Sensitivity and Awareness in the Classroom.* Cambridge, Mass.: Howard A. Doyle Publishing Co., 1966.

CHAPTER 4

Authentic and Unauthentic Learning

My intention in this chapter is to discuss the significance of self-awareness, personal involvement, and authentic relatedness as essential values in learning and to differentiate characteristics of alienation and betrayal that result in distortion and inauthenticity. I shall begin with Steve, a fourth-grade youngster who was consistently bored in school.

Steve spent nearly all of his time in the classroom noting, recording, and memorizing "facts" in various subject areas and listening to endless, dull lectures. What little excitement his teacher generated came from the exuberance she expressed when youngsters turned in "perfect" papers. Successful achievement in discrete subject matter, facts, and skills was the most important goal in school. To reach this goal, the teacher stuck faithfully to teachers' manuals, lesson plans, and textbooks. Each day was organized and structured like every other, and Steve was dead in school, numbed by the repetitive, uneventful activities and routines. Only the recess period enabled him to escape the monotony of the classroom and to give himself completely to football, basketball, or baseball.

Although his life in school was one of indifference and boredom, outside of school he became fully absorbed in a number of interests. He was dedicated to search and inquiry and would exhaust himself in one interest until he was satisfied and ready to move on. An illustration of his dedication was his complete involvement in astronomy for about six months. While strolling along the seashore one night, he really noticed the stars, as if for the first time. He sat on a rock and listened and watched until he was totally immersed in the sky. He was so fully engaged in the experience that he seemed to be in a trance.

Some weeks later in school, in science class, the assigned topic was "planets and constellations." While his teacher moved in and out of this topic in the usual efficient and perfunctory manner, Steve's experience at the ocean was reawakened, and he stayed with the stars for the rest of the school year. His involvement was so evident that even his teacher caught glimpses of this special light, but she made no effort to respond. For a while his whole world was a world of sun and satellites and planets. In school he went through the motions of completing assignments, but he was not actually there. His mind was exploring the heavens nearly all of his waking hours. He prodded and badgered his parents and the librarians for references, maps, telescopes, and trips to science museums and the local planetarium. For many, many weeks he could be seen nightly with telescope in hand, studying the constellations of stars and checking his reference books for seasonal changes. He began to understand the solar system, theories about its origin, the nature of auroras, comets, meteors, and eclipses; he knew, from his own enthusiastic search, details about each planet—size, shape, age, weight, distance from sun and earth, and temperatures; he was especially caught up in the stars, and could differentiate constellations of spring, summer, autumn, and winter; and he was entranced for long periods with galaxies and magnitudes. Every evening he reported his newest discoveries in exciting comments and challenges to his family. Eventually, he aroused his parents and siblings to join him in his search and to share his world of ecstasy. For Steve, the stars were an authentic interest, from who knows what integration of experiences and resources. He immersed himself totally in this interest for a while, often exhausting his energies and stretching his capacities. He involved important people in his world in it, until he experienced a sense of fulfillment, a letting go, and was ready to move on to other interests and activities.

If learning is to be meaningful and genuine, children must be free to remain with that which interests them and provokes involvement and collaboration. Strange as it may seem, when such an opportunity is afforded in the classroom, the child does not remain fixed in a single interest; having exhausted his enthusiasm, satisfied his curiosity, and experienced a sense of fulfillment, he ventures into new life, but he takes with him an innovating experience and he is reborn. Self-interest and absorption in subject matter are essential aspects of authentic learning. Without the presence of the authentic self of the learner, learning is meaningless and inconsequential.

Self-Communion and Meditation

Another way to significant learning is through self-communion and meditation. In such moments, the person is in touch with himself, and by following the cues of his own senses, he stays on the path of his individuality and remains true to his own destiny. In the moment of experience and activity, he knows who he is and where he is going. An excerpt from Loren Eiseley's book, *The Mind As Nature* [2], expresses the value of the solitary search for meaning:

> In Bimini, on the Old Spanish Main, a black girl once said to me: "Those as hunts treasures must go alone, at night, and when they find it, they have to leave a little bit of their blood behind."
> I have never heard a finer, cleaner estimate of the price of wisdom. I wrote it down at once under a sea lamp, like the belated pirate I was, for the girl had given me unknowingly the latitude and longitude of a treasure —a treasure more valuable than all the aptitude tests of this age.

In meditation, the person does not force thoughts to come, nor does he dwell on the usual fixations. He simply waits until he is in touch with the vital dimensions of his own self. The individual empties his mind of all thought and permits the significant feelings, perceptions, and visions to emerge and his real consciousness of nature and life to grow and expand. He allows himself to make genuine contact with the important dimensions of his world. In order to achieve the meditative experience, when the individual is at one with his real self, it is often necessary to experience a feeling of physical relaxation and to use one's own powers of concentration.

Peerbolte [10] suggests the following:
1. Sit in a comfortable armchair.
2. Place feet on the ground and extend arms along the armrests.
3. Sit easily and quietly.
4. After doing this simple exercise for a few minutes each day, start concentrating on the right arm during the exercise (left-handed people should concentrate on the left arm). Ask yourself whether this arm is quite at rest. Generally, it will be observed that there are some muscle tensions and contractions in the arm, even when one tries to deepen the feelings of rest.
5. After practicing this exercise for several weeks twice a day for one to five minutes, a feeling of lassitude and heaviness will be experienced in the arm. This is an indicator of the arm's relaxation.

At no time should willful efforts be made to provoke the sense of relaxation and heaviness. These preliminary exercises are aimed at bodily relaxation and can be achieved in many other ways, beginning, perhaps, with one part of the body in which the individual is most tense. Through the use of physical exercise aimed at relaxation of bodily tensions and concentration and awareness of one's bodily self, a climate or mood is created in which the individual is open to the meditative experience.

Being alone with one's self enables the person to reflect on his experience, to perceive and examine the parameters of a real issue or problem, and to engage openly and freely in thought and feeling. At the same time, there is a letting go, so that images and thoughts move in and out until a single dimension emerges, which becomes the center of intensive exploration. Through meditation, new facets of the self enter awareness, and opportunities for growth and development are revealed. To be in touch with one's self means that the person knows life from his own senses; he is rooted in his own existence, and he discovers reality and meaning from the knowledge of his own experience. The individual must—to learn validly—be a self in these ways: First, he must be open to himself and open to the world. Second, he must be free to choose and select from the vantage point of his own capacities, talents, and resources, in terms of the person he is. Third, he must be courageous enough to confirm the fitting and deny the nonfitting; in other words, to say "yes" to some of life's possibilities and ventures and "no" to others. Finally, he must take the responsibility for his choices and actions, learning from mistakes, not being fixed by them or distorted by them, but using them as steps in a journey where a temporary detour has interfered with forward movement and progress, and yet where the delay is an essential part of the experience—and learning, too, from right choices that confirm decision and action and make possible continuing growth and formation of self-enhancing attitudes and values. Freedom of choice is necessary to gain a sense of self-esteem and to develop sources of inner strength with which to face new problems or challenges, with which to live with frustration, defeat, or crisis, and stay with the threat or peril without being broken or destroyed by it.

Authentic Relationship to One's Self

If learning is to be other than a series of abstractions or isolated facts, it is essential that the individual be challenged by real issues and problems, by subject matter that engages the learner, captures his attention, and absorbs him. The individual, if he is authentic, contemplates life and makes choices for search and study on the basis of his own desires, interests, and talents, not out of a need for approval or reward or status, not out of ambition and striving for power, or a need to win out over others. The challenge of authentic choice is a real challenge today because the values of the school and society are, in many respects, geared to successful achievement and a high place in the social hierarchy. Thus, being genuine requires courage to stand by one's own self in the face of pressures to conform to the standards and expectations of others. This was the kind of courage shown by Chibi in Yashima's sensitive portrayal of a boy in school struggling to maintain a growing sense of identity in the face of an impersonal system of education [17].

Chibi fights to stay alive in school as an individual by engaging in self-reflection, meditating in class, and remaining in touch with his own experiences. He is constantly rebuked, punished, and rejected by his teachers, and is considered odd and stupid by his peers. Chibi's response to the rejection is to withdraw more and more into his lonely world of sounds and images and visions, to relate to the natural life that surrounds him, and to become increasingly afraid of teachers and children in school. Chibi learns to combat the ugly faces and gestures by ignoring them, seeing only what he wants to see and hearing only what he wants to hear. Just the ceiling or the wooden top of his desk is interesting enough for him to watch for hours. A patch on a boy's shoulder is something to contemplate and study. And outside the window are exciting things to see and follow and learn from all year long. Chibi can hold and watch insects and grubs that teachers and children are repelled by. He can imagine and dream and wonder and follow his thoughts freely to a point of new awareness and meaning. The years of school life pass by quickly, and while other children are being drilled, are conforming and becoming numb to inner life, Chibi keeps right on growing as a self and keeps alive the images in his eyes and the dreams in his heart. He learns to know the places where wild grapes and wild potatoes grow. He learns how to recognize, care for, and cultivate the flowers in the class garden; he learns how to write in a style that is his own, and because it is not the standard form, it is not easily read by anyone but Chibi; he learns to make vivid black and white drawings that depict the life that surrounds him. Finally, he meets a teacher who enters his world, values his uniqueness and creativity, and invites him to contribute his own style and background of experience to the activities of the school. The day arrives when Chibi is on the stage of the school facing the audience of parents and teachers and peers who have belittled and maligned him over the years. Chibi imitates the voices of crows—sounds from the newly hatched crow, the voices of a mother crow and a father crow, the cry of the crow early in the morning, in a time of crisis and tragedy, the call of gaiety and happiness, and the far and lonely cry of the crow, which is Chibi's own voice calling out from the far mountainside, yearning and hungry for genuine human contact. These are Chibi's voices of encounter with life when he is shut off from human companionship; these are calls of awareness and differentiation of the life of crows, which he has learned through sensitive listening over six years of walking daily miles and miles to his school from his mountain village, leaving home at dawn and not arriving back again until sunset. It takes a shocking performance to awaken the grown-ups and children to a recognition of Chibi's individuality, his industrious and ingenious nature, and the basic richness of life that is still in contact with beauty and simplicity, of life that is genuinely and uniquely alive and responsive to a world of varied themes and sights and colors and fragrances.

Similar experiences are described in Saint-Exupery's *The Little Prince* [13]. A boy of six, fascinated by stories about life in a primeval forest, ponders deeply the adventures of the jungle and draws a picture of a boa constrictor digesting an elephant. To his disillusionment, grown-ups see the drawing merely as a hat, and so the boy, undaunted but discouraged, draws a second picture—eliminating something of the aesthetic value but offering more clues and clearly depicting the elephant inside the snake. The main response of adults is to advise the little prince to give up his drawing and devote himself to geography, history, arithmetic, and grammar. He learns that grown-ups never understand anything by themselves and that children must forever be explaining things to them. For a while he forsakes sharing his thoughts and dreams of boa constrictors, primeval forests, and stars; he learns to talk about bridge, golf, and politics; and he is regarded as an unusually sensible young man.

It is extremely difficult to stay on a path of meaningful living, because the path is constantly being invaded, confounded, and shifted by people who have no awareness or sensitivity for what is involved and who mix their own desires, needs, and purposes into the life of the other in such a way that it becomes a burden to unravel one's own real perceptions from those aimed at mollifying, appeasing, and influencing others. What should be the natural and simple way—being honest with one's self and being involved in genuine interests and activities—has become terribly complicated. Individuals no longer know where they are going and what they want from life. Being authentic is not a matter of degrees, not a quantitative distinction; rather, it is an ingredient of being. A person either is himself or is not himself; he either is rooted in his existence or is a counterfeit, he either is living authentically or is caught up in a world of masks and roles and status symbols.

The first relationship essential to learning and developing is the relationship to one's own self. This involves being open to one's own potentials and resources; engaging in a process of meditation or contemplation that leads to self-awareness, attention, and concentration; making choices that are consistent with one's own desires, purposes, and capacities; and having the courage to stand by principles and values that grow out of the validation and actualization of good choices.

Unless the individual bases his experience on inner truth and authenticity, on real interests, desires, and purposes, on perceptions that enhance a particular identity, he becomes a counterfeit. Without authentic presence to one's self, the individual is actually communicating as a double, and the pretense will color and distort problem-solving, knowledge, and understanding of real issues and controversies. The steps involved in growth of the self are the existence of a problem or issue that captures the learner's attention, or the presence of a desire or interest that encourages self-expression and activity; the opportunity for uninterrupted meditation or silent dialogue; the availability of resources in the form of maps, books, audio-visual and other materials, instruments and equipment, and people who can be consulted at appropriate moments along the way; freedom to act on and confirm or reject hunches, possibilities, and assumptions, and the use of resources that actually contribute to the process.

Any situation in which the individual is confronted with a variety of possibilities, alternatives, or resources involves the self. For example, in the classroom, the child may choose from a diverse group of colors, shapes, or forms; he may choose from a number of references within a subject area or from different subject areas; he may choose also the way to proceed—self-reflection, dialogue, appropriate adult resources; he may choose from among interests and activities; he may choose from among aesthetic, intellectual, or spiritual materials, goals, and purposes. If learning is to be imaginative, creative, and productive, it must stem from a real person, engaging in self-searching, exploration, awareness, and decision or action. In other words, knowledge that is integral to the self of the learner leads to convictions, beliefs, opinions, and values; feelings lead to preferences, interests, satisfactions, and pleasure or displeasure. Through authentic involvement, the individual learns which experiences to pursue and which to abandon; he also learns which aspects of the world offer genuine challenge for elaboration and emphasis.

John—to Paint or Not to Paint Freely

The significance of self-encounter and authentic presence is illustrated in the experience of John, who struggled for weeks to free himself from the restraints of conformity, from schedules and time pressures and the expectations, standards, and demands of parents and teachers. Here was a person with unusual capacities, yet he was extremely fearful of venturing into unknown areas or exploring new experiences or experimenting with new materials or ideas. In school, John was an outstanding student in terms of achievement and grades. He was referred for child therapy by his parents, who had become anxious and disturbed (though they had significantly contributed to the pattern) as John increasingly conformed and withdrew into a docile and passive pattern, even where protest was warranted and desirable; they became concerned that this bright, talented boy was using his resources to adjust to the requirements of others; they were also disturbed by his lack of a sense of adventure and his extreme agitation and anxiety in approaching any new experience, whether introduced gradually or suddenly.

The split in John and in his world came sharply into focus, plaguing and tugging at him, when he faced himself in the challenge of painting or not painting freely. For weeks, in therapy, he had painted according to the same procedures: getting ready, arranging paper and paints, making a plan, then proceeding precisely and with caution to follow the prescription. During this time he did not paint spontaneously, nor was there any enthusiasm or excitement in what he made. He followed a carefully organized plan, painting efficiently and following his own directions in a methodical way. He usually had difficulty deciding what to paint and attempted to get direction from his therapist, but once he realized he would have to struggle with the problem himself and make his own decisions, he became deeply distressed, painfully weighing different possibilities. After many minutes of unsteady and uncertain deliberation, he decided to paint items in the playroom and scenes in nature. Mechanically and joylessly he outlined and copied. When his therapist made no value judgments on the finished products, John would approach his mother for support. The themes of the paintings were usually pastoral scenes, with plenty of sunshine, flowers, smoke from chimneys, and tall, growing grass—yet the themes of all his other activities in therapy were aggressive or hostile, involving killing, shooting down, attacking, and attempting to eliminate. As he became freer, more comfortable, and more open and spontaneous in therapy, the stereotyped, structured, and modeled paintings no longer satisfied him. For a long time he did not paint at all. Then one day he had a strong desire to paint but was stuck on how to begin and what to begin with. After many minutes of self-confrontation in which he rejected a number of ideas, he said, "I'll just start and see what happens." From that day, he painted nearly every week, without purpose or plan but with a feeling of spontaneity and zest and openness in which he and the painting were related. There was a noticeable change, not only in his expansive use of color, shading, and movement, but in the entire scene. In contrast to the earlier silent, heavy, serious caution, John experienced an increasing sense of abandonment and freedom to explore and test; he improvised and invented as he went along; his whole body was involved, not just his arms and fingers. There were moments when he seemed to be within the painting, totally absorbed and immersed in the experience, and working very hard to integrate the free flow of the paint with motions of his body and the rapid, fleeting ideas of his mind. Along with the variations in color and movement, the silent burden of painting had become alive with sound—gleeful voice expressions and sighs of joy. Often John talked back to his paintings, engaging in exciting, running dialogue. At first, he labeled the new art expressions his "nonpaintings," but with each new experience he approached recognition and ownership of his work and pride in it. Eventually, he valued this spontaneous, free art and affirmed it as real painting in contrast to the earlier copying and modeling. In one of his last paintings, he recognized his growth and at last could say of his work, "Just a little bit of sunshine breaking through the pinhole of a needle." The feel was right; John still had a way to go to freedom, genuine choice, and authentic self-expression; but he was on his way, and there was more of John in the movement of his body, in the rhythmical sound of his footsteps and in his wonderful, sparkling talking back to himself.

Children face many challenges in life, many issues and conflicts that require self-reflection, struggle, and resolution. Every child knows the tragedy of separation and death, the feeling of being loved one moment and abandoned the next, a sense of isolation and loneliness; every child witnesses and feels the impact of battle, argument, hostility, and the shifts in mood and sudden crises that, in some ways, affect and alter his relationship to himself and to the significant people in his world and cause him to doubt the people he lives with and sometimes loves. The child needs time to be alone when his world is threatened or shattered. He needs time in his own solitude to feel what is happening in him and to remain sensitive and aware.

Every person also experiences euphoric, peak moments that transcend lesser times and leave the person alive, vibrant, and joyous—emotions that require time to be with and savor, emotions that place the individual in a world of wonder and fancy that separates him from others and sends him soaring. It is important that the person keep these dreams alive, that he follow these visions of his heart to a point of fulfillment. To do this the person must have opportunity to meditate and lose himself in dreams and forests and stars, in imagination and fantasy. For a while, the individual must plunge into timeless experience and let his world be filled in all its facets with the euphoric, great moments or the painful, despairing times. If he can live within these moments, he will maintain an authentic relationship to himself and to his world; he will emerge from the experience renewed as a human being and will bring with him sensitivity, awareness, and feeling that will cast rays of light and meaning into everything he undertakes.

Betrayal and Alienation

The most significant condition hindering genuine learning and development may be summed up by one word—betrayal. Betrayal exists in many forms, but basically it involves a deviation from one's own real self and unintentional or deliberate suppression of real feelings and perceptions in favor of substitute, counterfeit forms. It is motivated by a need to manipulate and exploit and is sometimes justified in the name of love or as an escape from disapproval and rejection. Betrayal is an act of self-rejection, the killing of one's own feelings in order to achieve status and success, the willingness to wear masks and engage in pretenses for the sake of safety and security. Any act of betrayal is essentially a lie, and the real person behind the lie moves significantly toward renunciation and alienation. Adjustment is a form of betrayal, because, in order to win approval, the individual distorts and denies a whole range of unique emotions, preferences, interests, and ways of relating. The individual gives up his own self and takes on the habits, expectations, and patterns of speech and behavior of others.

In a thought-provoking essay on violence and love, R. D. Laing [6] expresses the belief that from the moment of birth the infant is subjected to forces of violence, called love, that destroy potentialities for genuine learning and development. Love, properly speaking, is an absolute valuing of the other person, a letting be, and a feeling of wonder in the presence of this unique being. According to Laing, what is called love in human society is basically an exploitation of the other person, an attempt to constrain the individual's freedom, to force the other person to act on our perceptions, judgments, and standards, and a basic indifference to the individual's own existence and destiny. What happens in the process? Laing puts it this way:

> The result of our adjustment to our society is that having been tricked out of our minds, that is to say, out of our personal world of experience, out of that unique meaning with which potentially we may endow the external world, we have been simultaneously conned into the illusion that we are separate "skin-encapsulated egos." . . .
> The others have installed themselves in our hearts, and we call them ourselves. Each person, not being himself either to others or to himself, just as others are not themselves to themselves or to us, neither recognizes himself in the other, nor the other in himself. Hence being at least a double essence, haunted by the ghost of his own murdered self, no wonder modern man is addicted to other persons, and the more time he spends with others, the more lonely he becomes.
> There is a further twist of the tourniquet. For now, love becomes a further alienation, a further act of violence. My need is a need to be needed, my longing is a longing to be longed for. I act now to install what I take to be myself in what I take to be the other person's heart.

Betrayal begins with self-rejection, which itself begins with rejection by others. The person not only has been destroyed as a unique, authentic self by the rejection of others, but knowingly or unknowingly, he has participated in the process by rejecting himself. The betrayal of self-rejection may be direct and within the awareness of the individual or it may be devious and duplicitous. Sometimes adults program the child's life with incentives and rewards, so that he progresses step by step toward their expectations and standards. In the process, the unique child is canceled out, and what emerges is a social robot that takes its direction from external judgments and cues. In other words, the real self of the child is eliminated from existence.

When betrayal of the self occurs through duplicity, the individual is caught in a double bind. The message communicated by parents and teachers is twofold and contradictory. Outwardly these adults say they respect the child's own perceptions, interests, and preferences, but at the same time another message is conveyed; namely, that they prefer and expect the child to conform to their own wishes and standards. Outwardly the words sound affirmative and accepting, but inwardly there is a range of bodily tensions and meanings that also register in the child's world. Duplicity enters the situation and is a form of betrayal when parents and teachers do not say what they mean—that is, they say one thing but mean another—or when thoughts and feelings are in opposition in the same person, or when any double, contradictory series of messages is being communicated from adult to child.

Out of numerous duplicitous interactions, the individual becomes increasingly separated from himself and becomes vulnerable and susceptible to manipulation and control in any direction. Without roots and a firm set of values, he is subject to the whims, wiles, and demands of others and can be easily directed toward destructive purposes and ends. A trenchant example of betrayal involving the breakdown of morality in a young child is depicted in *The Man Who Loved Children* (15). The illustration is taken from the afternoon visit of a young girl to the home of a neighbor. The old woman appears suddenly in front of the child, and running ahead, she turns every few steps to smile, nod, and beckon. Through a series of skillful maneuvers and the promise of future treats, she induces Louise to kill her cat.

The love that the old woman felt for Louise was love that long ago had come to mean exploitation, deceit, and betrayal. Louise was willing to trade words of praise and endearment and the promise of a future treat (which for her were indices of love) for violence, malice, and evil. Thus, both child and adult participated in the duplicity, each bargaining for the services of the other and each perpetrating the lie that pervaded their meeting and betrayed the real meaning of love and the real value of human relationship.

Implications for the Teacher

What are the implications of authenticity, freedom, and encounter for the teacher? First of all, the teacher must remove his professional mask and stop playing professional roles. This will not be easy, since much of his security comes from professional definitions and functions that tell him what to do, where to do it, and how. Abandoning the professional prescription and plan will leave the teacher open and vulnerable, as any authentic human being is. Only the phony role-player or the robot is impervious and employs fixed movements and actions based on mechanics, rules, and laws. Being a genuine person means that the teacher will meet each situation as a human challenge, with all the accompanying contingencies, uncertainties, and risks. In other words, in place of the earlier role-playing, professional jargon, and dictates of the system, which give a certain sense of security, the teacher will depend on himself, on his own perceptions and meanings as they emerge in concrete situations with children, other teachers, parents, and administrators. The human teacher uses his special training and experience as it fits, but his awareness is based on the real persons he encounters, not on tests, instruments, textbooks, and other authorities. In other words, his decision of what is needed to enable an individual to come to terms with problems or issues or to develop interests or talents is based on the specific person involved, in a specific culture at a particular time. Understanding follows concrete, meaningful experience; it grows out of knowledge that comes from direct encounters.

The professional background of the authentic teacher does not stand out as a dominant, controlling power. Rather, professional experiences become integrated within the teacher as a person; and these experiences should enable the teacher to be more sensitive, more perceptive, more expansive as a human being, and therefore more able to' use his own capacities, abilities, and knowledge. Rather than rushing in with a quick diagnosis and plan, which has an authoritarian, professional ring, the authentic teacher waits and listens and enters into the classroom situation as a real person. He lets himself go and forms his understanding on the basis of his actual experiences; he does not offer resources or suggestions until he fully knows the unique requirements of the particular persons involved. The awareness of what is required comes from his own freedom of being, his direct involvement and interest, and his willingness to follow the leads of his own senses, both in the situation and in his own solitude and meditation. The authentic teacher increasingly becomes who he is in each relationship, facing problems and seeing possibilities for new life, possibilities for creative, meaningful activity. He offers these possibilities as alternatives, as potentially constructive solutions, but he accepts and values the right of the other person to find his own way. The teacher makes himself available and offers alternatives and resources but continues to respect the interests, judgments, and preferences of others. If he is a specialist at all, it is in enabling others to use their capacities and skills for healthy living and for meaningful experience. This does not come from diagnosis, prescription, and lesson plans; it comes from the teacher's awareness, involvement, and encounters with children, from the direct, primary experience of living with children, from steeping oneself in the worlds of children and letting genuine directions emerge. For the authentic teacher, a plan for a child comes through direct participation and involvement, through hours and hours of listening, through conversation and real dialogue, and through self-reflection and deliberation. Then the plan emerges, and since each of the persons involved helps to create it, it is a natural consequence of genuine meeting rather than a preconceived, dictating guide.

The moment for initiating an authentic life and departing from betrayal and alienation is always present. No matter how entrenched the teacher has been in professional labels, definitions, and classifications; no matter how fervently or listlessly he has played his role; no matter how often he has hidden behind dehumanizing diagnosis and analysis; no matter how mechanically he has engaged in flat intellectualizations; he still can decide to alter his way of meeting others in the school setting, and can discover a more meaningful and genuine basis for involvement. He still can become the one he really is, and can actualize his potentialities as a whole, unified person. Regardless of past associations or fixations, the teacher can begin to view life freshly, can once more be in touch with the imaginative and creative resources of his own real self, can participate in the lives of other people as an authentic human being, open and aware of real meanings and values. The choice is a difficult one to make, and the risk is often great, but the vitality and life that return when genuine talents and resources are used contain their own special merits and rewards. These come in the form of renewed zest and the good feeling of being rooted in one's self and knowing that one's footsteps are actually one's own. It is true that for every teacher at any moment he can choose to become himself, a unique person whose professional experiences and skills are integrated into his total being. The moment for considering such a choice is now, when anesthesia, dehumanization, fragmentation, and alienation are at a peak in the modern school.

REFERENCES

1. Bateson, Gregory, Jackson, Don D., Haley, J., and Weakland, John. "Toward a Theory of Schizophrenia," *Behavioral Science*, I (1956), 251–264.
2. Eiseley, Loren. *The Mind As Nature*. New York: Harper and Row, 1962.
3. Ewald, Carl. *My Little Boy/My Big Girl*. Translated by Beth Bolling. New York: Horizon Press, Inc., 1962.
4. Frankl, Viktor E. *Man's Search for Meaning*. New York: Washington Square Press, Inc., 1963.

5. Horney, Karen. "Finding the Real Self," *Amer. J. Psychoanal.,* IX (1949), 3–27.
6. Laing, R. D. "Violence and Love," *J. of Existentialism,* V (1965), 417–422.
7. Moustakas, Clark. *The Authentic Teacher: Sensitivity and Awareness in the Classroom.* Cambridge, Mass.: Howard A. Doyle Publishing Co., 1966.
8. Moustakas, Clark. *Creativity and Conformity.* Princeton, N.J.: D. Van Nostrand Co., 1967.
9. Pasternak, Boris. *Dr. Zhivago.* New York: Pantheon, 1958.
10. Peerbolte, M. Lietaert. "Meditation for School Children," *Main Currents in Modern Thought,* XXIV (1967), No. 1, 19–21.
11. Rogers, Carl. "Learning To Be Free," (Parts I and II) *Pastoral Psychol.,* XIII, No. 128, 47–54, and XIII, No. 129, 43–51.
12. Rogers, Carl. "A Theory of Therapy, Personality, and Interpersonal Relations as Developed in the Client-Centered Framework." In Sigmund Koch (ed.), *Psychology: A Study of Science,* Vol. 3. New York: McGraw-Hill Book Co., Inc., 1959.
13. Saint-Exupery, Antoine de. *The Little Prince.* Translated by Katherine Woods, New York: Harcourt, Brace, and World, 1943.
14. Salinger, J. D. *Nine Stories.* New York: New American Library, 1954.
15. Stead, Christina. *The Man Who Loved Children.* New York: Holt, Rinehart and Winston, 1965.
16. Weiss, Frederick A. Self-Alienation: Dynamics and Therapy. *Amer. J. Psychoanal.,* XXI (1961), 207–218.
17. Yashima, Taro. *Crow Boy.* New York: Viking Press, 1955.

CHAPTER 5

Essential Conditions in the Development of the Self

Every person, from the moment of birth, is a unique individual, unlike any other being who has ever existed. From the environment, nourishment and care are required to satisfy biological needs and to maintain life, but no individual is rooted solely in physical requirements, waiting passively to be aroused to states of tension, and then actively seeking to reduce these tensions and achieve a state of rest. From the very beginning, the infant reaches out into the world, alert, active, directed, expressive. Congenital activity and other signs of preference and selectivity are forerunners of imitation and later identity [4]. Sensory nerve endings, everywhere in the body, provide a basis for kinaesthetic, tactile, and internal experiences, as well as visual and auditory experiences. Helen Lewis [7] discusses the original self of the infant, as follows: ". . . a core of self-feeling is already his, i.e., feelings from within and

---

[1] Reprinted, with revisions, from Bulletin No. 19-A, *Children and Today's World*, Copyright 1967, by permission of the Association for Childhood Education International, 3615 Wisconsin Avenue, N.W., Washington, D. C. 20016.

from the surface of his body which can be considered the most fundamental experiences of a human being and which . . . actually form a core of his sense of self. . . . I am assuming that at no time is there an absence of differentiation between self and environment, that body and self-feeling exist from the beginning of infancy."

The first condition for creative emergence and expansion of self is already present at birth—namely, the freedom to be. Freedom is indicated in the spontaneous expressions of the infant—perceptions, movements, sensations, contacts with the immediate world. It is present as a natural process of life. The infant meets reality on his own terms and relates to his surroundings with his own resources. From the start, there is a free flow of life out into the world and a return. Already "yes" and "no" are in the infant's responses to life; there is confirmation of the fitting through harmony of contact, or denial of the nonfitting through refusal and avoidance. Day by day the infant's world, originally made up of fleeting movements and perceptions, becomes more distinct and varied. Having got over the shock and stress of the birth experience, he begins to take active note of the world. His eyes span broader horizons; his ears pick up distant sounds; he turns, touches, explores, experiments, savors and avoids. Gardner Murphy [11] describes the infants' world as a process of reaching out, relating, and discovering:

> They will immerse themselves in the world; they soak themselves in its rich qualities. Its endless problems and challenges are intrinsically appealing. Now and then it hurts them, and they learn how to avoid the recurrence of such hurts; but in general it is a rich and commanding world which they must understand and with which they must come to terms. Often the child has to be dragged from his sensory and motor satisfactions to swallow the food which adults think necessary to meet his "primary needs," or dragged to bed against the competition of excitations which stimulate his sense organs and later his imagination. Human nature, as directly observed, is no matter of viscera alone. It is a matter of exploring the possibility of surfaces, lines, colors, and tones and, later on, the symphonies, mountains and stars.

In a sense, these confirming and denying encounters with life represent early forms of choice. Selectivity based on organismic wisdom is a vital attribute of beginning life and is essential in the enhancement of individuality and authentic relatedness. Schachtel [14] has emphasized the self-actualizing values of infant sensations and perceptions:

> There is nothing sadistic in learning to bite by feeling pleasure. . . . There is nothing primarily sexual in the pleasure of the infant's grasping, with mouth or hands, of the mother's breast or in the pleasurable contacts with teddy bear, soft blanket, shaggy dog. There is nothing inherently aggressive in banging the rattle against a blanket or side of a crib or the spoon against the table, or in tearing paper. All these and many other vital sensations or fused perceptions which occur in the course of motor activity leading to the infant's pleasurable contact with environmental objects are essential steps in the infant's self-actualization; they furnish an important link in the infant's motivation for the continued exercise of its muscles and senses; its motor coordination, and its exploration of the environment as well as of its own body and physical capacities. . . . In contrast to Freud's relief-pleasure resulting from the attempt to get rid of the stimulus, the feeling of pleasure in sensory contact with environmental objects is in animal and man a tie to reality. . . . it plays a stimulating role in the growing infant's and man's realization of his potentialities and in his total relatedness to the world.

Freedom of being and selectivity are self-realizing values that enable the infant to trust his own senses to lead to harmony and fit, and to cry out in protest against the thwarting, alienating dimensions of the environment. By his perceptual and sensual contacts and freedom of movement, he participates in life and creates a sense of well-being, continuity, and fulfillment. Rogers [12] postulates the following as characteristics of the human infant: (1) His *experience* of reality is his reality; (2) He has a greater potential awareness of what reality is for him than does anyone else in his environment; (3) His relationship to reality is based on his basic actualizing tendency; (4) In the interaction between infant and world, the infant expresses himself as an organized whole; (5) He engages in an *organismic valuing process,* positively valuing experiences that are enhancing and negatively reacting to those that are not; (6) He moves toward positively valued experiences and avoids those that are negatively valued.

Out of the original awarenesses, the infant and the young child begin to focus selectively and to include only what is relevant. Selective awareness becomes patterned perception as the individual learns to perceive and integrate what he is ready to recognize and value and relate to [5].

What begins as contact with the environment eventually becomes collaboration. The environment evolves and is transformed by the presence of the child, just as the child is creating and expanding with life. It is a kind of laboring together, like that of the farmer who initiates a process of change in the soil that eventually not only enriches the soil but yields an abundant, healthy crop.

Maslow [8] discusses the collaborative nature of the individual and society as a form of synergy. From his studies of free choice in different animal species and in human infants, he remarks, "We can say that these experiments demonstrate a synergetic working of . . . head and heart . . . in which our impulses lead us in a wise direction."

The human infant is not confronted with the problem of to be or not to be; he naturally and spontaneously makes contact with what his senses confirm or deny. Even if fleeting in their primitive forms, these contacts with the world are the precursory forms of genuine encounter. The infant's experience is either enhancing and self-realizing or it is not. And this depends partly on whether the significant persons in his world are trusting and affirmative.

As James Agee [2] puts it:
> In every child who is born, under no matter what circumstances, and of no matter what parents, the potentiality of the human race is born again, and in him, too, once more, and of each of us, our terrific responsibility towards human life; towards the utmost idea of goodness, of the horror of error, and of God.

> Every breath his senses shall draw, every act and every shadow and thing in all creation, is a mortal poison, or is a drug, or is a signal or symptom, or is a teacher, or is a liberator, or is liberty itself. . . .

Freedom and Choice Inherent in the Life Process

The first two conditions for the growth of the self—freedom and choice—are inherent in the process of life itself, in the qualities and expressions of the infant—the lusty cries, the alternating patterns of rest and activity, the cooing and gurgling, movements and facial gestures, openings and closings of eyes and body—all the varied expressions and thrusts of burgeoning life. Freedom and choice are the crux of existence, the difference between spontaneous, alert connections with the flow of life and controlled, mechanical projections; between continual building and expanding of self and static repetitions and fixations; the difference between continual emerging of new forms and routines fixed by the clock; between variety and diversity of expression and the rigid patterns of behavior conditioned through skillful manipulation of environment and strategic use of reward and punishment. Beyond the genetic pattern and original potentialities, freedom to be, spontaneity of contact, and immediacy of choice are the factors that enable total being to flourish and that permit tactile, auditory, and perceptual processes to emerge and grow.

Self-confirmation is the early form of responsibility. Through trusting his own organismic connection with life and his own senses to confirm or deny, the individual is taking charge of his life. In actualizing himself as a free being, the individual is fulfilling a basic or primary responsibility—to be who he is at any moment, to place himself authentically in the universe, and to accept the happenings and consequences. Errors are only temporary detours or blocks along the way to personal growth. They may hold the person for a while, but as long as the individual is not stuck by them, he will continue on to new forms of development and creation.

In the early development of the self, affirming the value of one's own experience comes first; recognition and valuing of others comes later. To continue to appreciate and respect his self, however, the individual is dependent upon the response of others. Though it is enhanced through parental recognition and love, the original self cannot be entirely destroyed. The original uniqueness and wisdom of the organism are capacities that can be exercised at any moment in making choices, in differentiating and refining features of the self, and in the process of growing an identity. Charlotte Buhler [3] found this to be true in her detailed study of 40 individuals in psychotherapy. She described the environmental backgrounds of these persons as rejecting, pressuring, distant, negligent, and morally objectionable. The emotional conflicts and problems of the group had much in common, yet their values and ways of life differed considerably. Buhler concluded that the person's own basic tendencies, that is, organismic patterns and directions, were more determinant in value choices than the dynamics of personal relations. By basic tendencies of life, Buhler is referring to four tendencies: *need satisfaction* (tendencies toward release, comfort, happiness), *self-limiting adaptation* (tendencies toward restricting or fitting in), *expansive creativity* (tendencies toward creativity and self-realization), and *upholding the internal order* (tendencies toward self-sustenance and integration).

Although emotional predicaments may impede freedom of choice, values continue to be chosen that are consistent with original basic tendencies. In other words, the individual's own uniqueness is a much more potent factor in the development of identity than the dynamics of early environmental conditioning. Buhler contends that "choice of identity and values bring out (from the start) more of the individual's own self than dynamics of learning account for, even at a time when the individual is under emotional impact and quite unfree." Although the four basic tendencies are primary components in the development of self-values, recognition and love from the environment play an important part in the beginning. The confirmation of others strengthens being and fosters spontaneity and vitality in self-expression. Through confirmation, increasing differentiation of the self occurs.

Choices and Decisions:
Preliminary Steps in Creation of Values

In the process of creating, refining, and establishing more definite and consistent self-forms, will and intention and desires are important in structuring experience and determining the direction of self-development. The individual, being free to be, makes choices and decisions affected by willing, feeling, thinking, and intending. Through self-awareness, the person enters situations already pointed or set in certain directions. Later, the experience of the individual in making choices is often based on conscious, self-determined thought and feeling. The making of choices that can be confirmed or denied in experience is a preliminary step in the creation of values. Choices that confirm being and lead to enriching and expanding self-awareness, that deepen experience and lead to new experience, and that challenge uniqueness and talent and lead to actualizations enable the person to establish further an identity that is authentic in itself and related to life. Ultimately, those choices that confirm life and enable the individual to become what he can be are chosen as values. Increasingly, the individual is growing and expanding in authentic ways; he is creating new awarenesses and values; he is coming to be what he can be in the light of opportunities and resources outside and potentialities and challenges inside.

Genuine meaning forms a bridge between self and other, between the person and the world, between subject and object, between the knower and the known. This is beautifully expressed by Ross Mooney [9]:

> as it is with a tree
> whose fitting task

ESSENTIAL CONDITIONS IN THE DEVELOPMENT OF THE SELF

    it is
to interknit the earth and sky
in one will drawn togetherness
of soil and sun,
as, from the deepest root,
a bit of earth is chosen,
taken, transformed, transported far
into the topmost tendril tip
to texture there
a newborn leaf,
joining into sky;
a motion matched,
in fitting need,
as from the highest leaf
a bit of sun-lit air is chosen,
taken, transformed, transported far
into the deepest fibril tip
to texture there
a newborn root,
joining into earth
to make the living tree
symbol of
THE FITTING ONE
that inter-living earth and sky
gives birth to wholeness on the way
and gives to me a birthplace too,
for emerging life in me,
as I stand among the trees
and let them knit
a universe
on a Sunday afternoon.

In this poem, Mooney has touched upon the elementary conditions of existence. These conditions are (1) *Belonging*. (The individual, through expanding sensitivity and range of movement, increasingly establishes connections with the universe. The individual exists in belonging in the universe and in himself.) (2) *Being*. (The individual, by continuing to respect himself as the center of his own experience, is able to realize his potentialities through increasing differentiation and identity.) (3) *Becoming*. (The individual, through expanding cognitive span and expanding action span, opens new possibilities for transactions with life.) (4) *Befitting*. (The individual expands the range of complexity of what is possible to fit. "What is included from the outside must be fitted to that which is included from the inside to make an emergent one. . . .")

Confirmation

From the beginning, the individual is *of* the world, as well as *in* the world. Certain environmental conditions play a significant part in the individual's destiny, in the development of a feeling of being related, of belonging, of intimacy and value. The confirmation of others, the existence of others as genuine persons, the presence of others as real—all have an impact on evolving life. Through being affirmed, the individual experiences a personal significance that gives vitality to existence. In the infant, there is a sense of well-being, a feeling of delight and wonder in the universe, a desire for further encounter, the joy of being oneself and stretching forward to new reaches of life. Thus, the first value in mother and child encountering is for the mother to cherish the unique presence and varied "expressivity" of her infant. Confirming the infant means trusting his own creative development, valuing his presence, and accepting his own pacing and timing of physical and existential needs. Basically, it means an assertion of "yes" to his own ways of being in the world.

Authentic Presence

Another way in which adults serve the growing child is through genuine presence, by being sources of life itself. The enriching parent enables the young child to develop new feelings, learn new patterns, and discover different ways of relating to life. The mother and child relationship evolves as the patterns of living of the two persons register in each other. A mother cannot be a real mother without confirmation from the infant, and the infant cannot develop his potentialities without confirmation from the mother. If the collaboration is a healthy one, individuality is enhanced and patterns of mutuality emerge. The significant adult must exist for the growing individual as all forms exist: he is simply there, as rocks or the sea are present; there, to be met, related to, and affected by; there, as a source for developing awareness and relationship. A mother can have a significant impact on the developing child, without any intent to manipulate or change him. In this sense, the mother is being herself, not in order to influence, yet the way she is has relevance for the growing child. It is the difference between being-in-itself and being-in-order-to; between experience for itself and planned activity in order to change. If I happen to be influenced by another person because something in him resonates with something in me, which enables me to see or be in a different way, that is a very different reality from the deliberate effort of another to induce me to become what he thinks I should become.

The individual will learn social values through encounters with significant adults, through identification, and through separation of the self from others. Whether he chooses social values because they confirm basic tendencies within himself depends upon the kind of being he is as well as the nature of his emotional experiences and ties to others. With reference to authentic relatedness, all the adult can do is be there, as an alive, genuine person. To the extent that this presence fits, it will have a bearing on the emerging feelings and values of the child. Thus, the individual, in a healthy climate of growth and development, will learn from others, beyond the social amenities and routines, certain values of the self—authenticity, sensitivity, gentleness, kindness, truth, and ways of genuine participation and joint effort. David Smillie [15] describes the bond between the infant and his world as follows:

> The world of the infant is initially one of belonging and relation. There is no separation of self and other, inner or outer, here or there. The world is the relation-

ship experienced; that is, a world of process and of being. To understand or describe this world we must recognize that the infant is dependent upon others in the sense that the roots of a tree are dependent on the trunk, as a bird's flight is dependent upon the air, as my movements depend upon my muscles. The world of the child is an organic unity in which the child as a self is an immanent aspect. To the extent that the mother enters into this world and becomes a part of it, the infant is dependent upon her as he is upon air to breathe and space to move. This is a dependence of mutuality including mother and child. For neither of them is there a necessity to orient themselves toward goals or to satisfy needs and desires. The only necessity is, like the dependence, the necessity to exist in an undifferentiated unity.

Providing Resources

A third way in which adults can constructively participate in the development of the child's self is by providing resources that are relevant to the child's own tendencies, preferences, or patterns of expression. By being sensitive to the child's enthusiasm and direction, the adult can make available resources: colors, shapes, forms, and materials to be tested, explored, and used in expanding perception and developing skills. Sometimes all that is required to bring a potential source of growth to a child is to point to it. Thus, the young individual sees what he has not seen before and confirms or denies its relevance as the situation demands. If he chooses it, it becomes part of his reality; it challenges further expression and self-actualization.

There is a basic difference between an arrangement of conditions and resources in the environment in order to direct and change, and an arrangement that has meaning in itself to the person who creates the situation. There is a difference between setting up objectives and goals aimed at altering the behavior of others in the direction of specific outcomes and making available materials and resources based on the preferences of the person, without any intent to influence. When the arrangement has value in itself, it is simply the way in which one self is authentically expressed in the presence of another self. The adult who arranges a situation as an invitation accepts as reality that it may not actually serve the other person, it may not be a way to self-realization for the other person, and he respects and appreciates the person's own choices.

When situations are arranged as invitations, even if it turns out that the resources become significant means to self-growth for the other person, the outcome is unknown and unpredictable. This is in contrast to the manipulative arrangement of environment, where purposes are specified and sought. In the first case, the arrangement and the person arranging are nonlineal; in the second, they are lineal. The nonlineal nature of environmental conditions is difficult to communicate, because our language is itself lineal. Dorothy Lee [6] observes the many, nearly automatic ways in which lineality is assumed to be a condition of reality:

> In our own culture, the line is so basic, that we take it for granted, as given in reality. We see it in visible nature, between material points, and we see it between metaphorical points such as days or acts. It underlies not only our thinking, but also our aesthetic apprehension of the given. . . . The line is found or presupposed in most of our scientific work. It is present in the *induction* and *deduction* of science and logic. . . . *We trace* a historical development; we *follow the course* of history and evolution *down* to the present and *up from* the ape. . . . When we see a *line* of thought, a *course* of action or the *direction* of an argument; when we *bridge* a gap in the conversation, or speak of the *span* of life or of teaching *a course,* or lament our interrupted career. . . . We . . . assume that the line is present in nature and, at most, to be discovered or given visual existence.

Because lineal implications of life between two persons are taken for granted, it is difficult to realize that a mother or father or any adult may structure conditions that have value and meaning as an outgrowth of a relationship with a child, without specific goals in mind. The resource may be presented without being connected to a goal, but simply as an addition to the environment, placed there as a result of cues from the child, to be chosen and encountered or not. Whether it will have meaning depends on his own perceptions, on its value for him.

Thus, it is in these ways that the human environment contributes to the development of genuine selfhood: first, through confirming the infant and young child as a being of noncomparable and nonmeasurable worth, in the individual's particular ways and as a whole; second, by being a living person, genuine, whole, present, open to encounter, available as a source of learning and enrichment; third, by making available resources based on the growing person's own interests, directions, and patterns of expression, resources that assist in extending and deepening experience, broadening horizons, and expanding reality by furthering interest and meaning.

REFERENCES

1. Agee, James. *A Death in the Family.* New York: Avon Books, 1959.
2. Agee, James, and Evans, Walker. *Let Us Now Praise Famous Men.* Boston: Houghton Mifflin Company, 1960.
3. Buhler, Charlotte. "Aiding the Patient to Find His Identity and the Values Consonant With It," *Psychotherapy: Theory, Research, and Practice,* II (1965), 89-91.
4. Buhler, Charlotte. *Values in Psychotherapy.* New York: Free Press, 1962.
5. Frank, Lawrence K. "Tactile Communication," *Gen. Psychol. Monog.,* LVI (1957), 209-225.
6. Lee, Dorothy. *Freedom and Culture.* Englewood Cliffs, N.J.: Prentice-Hall, Inc., 1959.
7. Lewis, Helen Block. "Over-Differentiation and Under-Individuation of the Self," *Psychoanalysis and Psychoanalytic Rev.,* XLV (Fall 1958), 3-24.
8. Maslow, Abraham H. "Synergy in the Society and in the Individual," *J. Individ. Psychol.,* XX (1964), 153-164.
9. Mooney, Ross. "The Elementary Conditions of Existence." Unpublished essay, Ohio State University, 1957.
10. Moustakas, Clark. *Creativity and Conformity.* Princeton, N.J.: D. Van Nostrand Co., 1967.
11. Murphy, Gardner. *Human Potentialities.* New York: Basic Books, Inc., 1958.

12. Rogers, Carl. "A Theory of Therapy, Personality and Interpersonal Relations As Developed In The Client-Centered Framework." In Sigmund Koch (ed.), *Psychology: A Study of Science*, Vol. 3. New York: McGraw-Hill Book Co., Inc., 1959.
13. Rogers, Carl. "Toward A Modern Approach To Values: The Valuing Process In the Mature Person," *J. Ab. and Soc. Psychol.*, LXVIII (1964), 160-167.
14. Schachtel, Ernest G. *Metamorphosis*. New York: Basic Books, Inc., 1959.
15. Smillie, David. "The Roots of Personal Existence," *J. of Humanistic Psychol.*, I (1961), 89-93.

CHAPTER 6

The Confrontation of Two Brothers

To illustrate the humanistic values and principles essential in personal growth, I have selected a recent experience with two brothers who had become alienated from each other following a severe family battle. The experiential process was the basis for reconciliation and growth.

As a person outside, yet related, I brought a new force into the relationship, a way of encouraging each person to remain in the path of the other and to keep the encounter vital and meaningful, in terms of real involvements and events. A climate was created in which the brothers could meet and face each other, struggle with the problems involved, and come to know the true meaning of their feelings and their relationships in the family. My intent was to keep open channels of communication; to initiate or invite a clear facing of the issues; and to reveal the underlying resentment, bitterness, and anger, as well as feelings of sympathy and love. The meeting was a genuine confrontation, for the brothers had not spoken to each other since the family battle. Though they were willing, even desirous, to examine the painful episode, neither knew how to begin, and both had fears that any effort at reconciliation would be blatantly rejected. Thus, a truce of alienated silence characterized their attitude as the meeting got under way.

Almost instantly I could feel the tension between them. They had arrived at different times from different directions; there was no greeting, no change in facial expression, no recognition of any kind; only detached silence, a cold stillness, and distance. Until the hostile dispute at home, they had been closer to each other than to anyone else in their lives, sharing a common world of hopes and dreams, and similar resentments and feelings. Many months ago, in a time of abject despair, Bill had remarked that no one really cared what happened to him but Steve: "When everything goes wrong, when I hate the world and everyone in it, I think of Steve because he's the only one who cares what happens to me."

Now, here they were—silent, shy, uncomfortable—each with eyes downcast. Slowly Bill's body slumped in the chair and he looked as if he were facing not just the end of the relationship, but the end of everything. The muscles of his body were strained and taut. From my previous meetings with him, I knew he was hanging on to the last threads of a bond that made the difference between the cold, crude, colorless day-by-day emptiness that made his existence a barren tragedy and the intense, expansive, warm, joyful feelings he experienced with his brother, the difference between the dark gloom that penetrated him and sudden, bright lights that turned him on inside and caused him to look at another person straight and realize that life had a meaning. In the past, he had described wonderful, rich moments with Steve when he was aware of himself; when he could feel the waves splashing against his body, the wind blowing through his hair, and the light of day in his heart; then he could notice, really notice, the face before him and feel inside himself that it was good to be alive, good just to be with another human being.

Steven—where was he now?—somewhere, far off, aloof, seemingly indifferent. Was he beyond a real meeting? Should I try to provoke him into dropping the mask? What was my responsibility in this hostile reunion?

How long we sat in the uncomfortable silence I do not know. Why didn't Bill speak? He had suggested the meeting, and now, there he was, stiff and withdrawn. He made no move to address either of us, but more and more, he turned away, with his face sharply averted and his body tightly fastened against his chair. Momentarily, I was annoyed, but only for a moment, for when I really looked at him I felt a deep concern for his suffering.

Although in subtle and devious ways the breach had been growing for some weeks, the fatal breakup of their friendship had just occurred, in an act of sudden rage and violence—on Bill's sixteenth birthday. Like all the birthdays he could remember, this one was a day he dreaded. Yet, at the same time, he yearned for it to come, because it meant freedom, new rights, and independence—not the birthday itself, but the symbol of growing up and being free, free from adult supervision and control and free from his parents' close surveillance. As the day approached, however, the terrors of the past were reawakened and incidents of long ago were strikingly real. A few days before his birthday, sitting next to me, following a long period of agitated silence, a look of anger crossed his face; his body stretched and twisted in pain. "No!" he screamed out—one shrill word, "No! No! No" The words were spoken in a fitful and spasmodic way; then he was dead silent. Suddenly, the whole atmosphere was frozen, and we sat in one still motion, feeling the agony together, unable to move or speak. This was no longer a young man before me but a transformed "thing," tormented by images and thoughts. He was gone, remote and isolated, and I was alone. At last I spoke to him, "Bill, what is it? What is happening? I want to help." After a long silence, he answered, "I can't get it out of my mind, I can't." *(Pause)* "Tell me about it, Bill. What's happening to you?" Then he started; with an almost impossible struggle, he spoke; he pulled at his nose, rubbed his eyes, and poked at his face—in a kind of lacerating rejection of himself. Strange sounds came from inside, and finally clear words.

"Have you ever gone back into time and felt something terrible happening to you, and you can't get rid of it? I'm thinking about my fifth birthday. We were at the lake, and people were shouting and playing around me. But I wasn't playing, I was watching or standing alone. Underneath I felt hatred for all those people. It wasn't my idea to come to the lake with them. They weren't my friends and they didn't care about me. Each time someone reminded me of my birthday I shouted and ran. *(Pause)* What is a birthday anyway? I don't know. Ever since I can remember I've hated that day—every hour of it; and I hated them too because they were part of it and because they were my mother's friends and not mine. In the dim background, I could hear their voices singing the birthday song. I laughed, and squealed and laughed again and again, mocking and teasing, 'I'll get the first piece of cake. Ha! Ha! Ha!' Then one voice, louder than the rest, pushed the others aside, and there she was towering over me—my mother. My own mother looking at me with hatred, and shrieking: 'You what? The first piece? Oh, yes. You want! Yes! Yes!' Her anger was so strong I thought she wanted to kill me. After a few moments of wild, hateful staring, she picked up the cake and smashed it against my head, rubbing the sticky frosting into my hair and into my eyes and ears and nose and mouth until I couldn't bear it anymore; screaming and running, running and crying, around in circles, nowhere to go—running, but where. No place to hide. At last I found a car and scrambled under it into a dirty, black hole."

Then he was weeping and shaking so hard he couldn't speak anymore. The painful sounds were utterly desperate and covered us both: "Oh, Bill, oh God, Bill, I'm sorry—terribly, terribly sorry." The crying stopped, but the pain continued, silently, for long, long minutes. In the the months he had been coming, he had never wept before me. For a while the stiff, set lines had disappeared, but now he was suddenly aware of his tears and the hard expression returned; he was battling against shame and humiliation, but he was also battling against the forces of life surging inside and trying to expel the mass of hatred and suffering. He hated his weeping. He hated his softening. He hated his own human response. This meant living again, and Bill wanted to bury life forever, to remain stationary and not venture forward. I sat up, struggling in the silence, fighting back my own tears—I looked up and found him; our eyes met for a moment. There he was, uncertainly but definitely moving toward me for the first time in our meetings. I knew he felt my deep caring, knew that it mattered to me that he had been brutally rejected and denied. Somehow, if it could all be canceled out and erased forever, I would gladly join him in the burial ceremony; but the scars were indelible, and only a new desire for life could overcome this crushing defeat of a self, only meaningful activity could transcend the decay and gloom that pervaded his world. For this moment, at least, he knew, he was sure, there was someone with him feeling deeply the agony of that fifth birthday—and all the other birthdays that destroyed his integrity and kept him imprisoned in a black pit of hatred and guilt. Once more I could see that meaning had to come from what we have known and what we have lived, and ours is always where we stand, as unique individuals. For Bill, "birthday" meant pain, conflict, rejection, violence, war, terror, flight, and loneliness.

But this was many weeks ago—when he relived the torture of that fifth birthday; now he was carrying the wounds of another birthday, his sixteenth year, a landmark for western youth. How great to step forward, I thought, and be slapped down again. Here he was, slumped low, hidden, tight, trying to be small, wanting to disappear—here he was, fleeing from a meeting that he himself had requested. He was moving further and further away from Steve and from me. At last, after what seemed an endless episode of quiet, desperate silence, I decided to interrupt, to begin with something direct enough to bring these brothers back into the same psychic sphere. Since Bill was clearly pleading to be left alone, I directed my remarks to Steve, although, of course, I was speaking to both of them.

"Steve, I think Bill wants to settle this issue between you. He asked for this meeting because he wants to be on good terms with you again. *(Pause)* He used to trust you and consider you his friend, but after the battle of last Monday he's afraid of you and no longer knows where he stands with you."

As I talked, Steve began to tighten. By the time I finished, he also had slumped back into a withdrawn state. Had my directness only succeeded in widening the gap? I waited. Although the situation grew even more tense for a few minutes, I felt that Steve was considering my remarks, struggling with his feelings, and deciding what he wanted to say. Slowly, he sat up, moved forward in his chair, and began to speak.

"The trouble with Bill is that he doesn't talk. This summer I've gone up to his room many times when I sensed he was unhappy or troubled. I've asked him what was bothering him. He won't answer. He clams up and says nothing or tells me to leave him alone. I'm getting disgusted. I'm ready to give up. *(Long pause)* Bill, why don't you talk with me when you have a problem?"

Bill moved slightly in his chair, and edged forward in the direction of his brother. He started to speak, then slumped back and moved away again. After a lengthy pause, Steve continued: "You see, you get no response from him. I don't know what's wrong with him. Last Monday he was yelling and smashing things in his room. I admit it. I couldn't take it anymore. I got so mad I tore in there and grabbed him and shoved him around. I feel sorry for what I did, Bill. But why don't you tell me what caused you to go berserk? I know you were disappointed and angry, but coming home and breaking furniture—that's acting like a baby. Say something, won't you! Help me to understand! What's this all about?" *(Long pause)*

Again Bill edged toward his brother, trying to form words. He rubbed his eyes and pulled on his nose and face, over and over again. The whole effort seemed doomed, a terrible, struggling agony and frustration. Steve waited, and then, irritated, went on: "Okay, so you won't talk. You're condemning your whole life, ruining your future. I don't want to be around when that happens. That's why I'm moving into an apartment soon. I'm fed up with all the bickering and fighting between you and them. I feel like a bystander watching a continual war. But if you think I'm on their side, you're mistaken. You're the one who matters to me, and your happiness. I wish you'd do something with your life—get out more often, make more of an effort with others, work harder in school, get better grades. How can I convince you that without an education you'll never be free of them. *(Long pause)* Bill, talk to me. Why did you go crazy that day and smash things? Tell me. Believe me, Bill, I don't want to see you hurt anymore."

Bill still did not speak, and Steve's agitation grew. "You see. I can't get through to him. I can't reach that kid. You can see why I'm ready to quit. Sometimes I think he enjoys being miserable." *(Long pause)*

"But, Steve, you have gotten through to him. He's listening to you but he's still unsure, and he's afraid. When you pinned him to a table and forced him to submit, he felt you had betrayed him."

"Well, what could I do—the banging and crashing he was doing and my mother's hysterical screaming finally got me. I lost control and grabbed him."

"Yes, I know, but Bill felt you were *against him*—not simply against what he was doing."

"I'm not against him. I never have been against him. If you don't hear anything else, hear this, Bill: *You* are the one at home I want to help. We're both of us alone in this world. All we've got is each other. Do you understand? I want to help!" Then suddenly, discouraged, Bill shouted: "Oh forget it; you don't believe me anyway."

Again, a long period of silence followed. Steve folded his arms; Bill was quiet and watchful. Once more, the distance increased, and a feeling of separation settled in. Once more, we were stuck in our own private worlds, drifting further away from each other. I interrupted the silence again.

"Steve, I would like to answer your question as to why Bill became angry and destroyed things last Monday. As you know, for months he had been waiting to take his driver's test and get his license. When he awoke Monday morning he felt great excitement, anticipating that within a few hours he would be permitted to drive without another licensed driver in the car. However, as the hour approached to take his test, he became more and more nervous and agitated. Your mother kept cautioning him, and just before going off with the patrolman she gave him a final warning: 'Beware of being ordered to make turns the wrong way on a one-way street.' In spite of this, the test went well for some time and his fears diminished. Unfortunately, as the test was nearing an end, the examiner suddenly ordered Bill to make a right turn. Bill was so shook up by the order that he saw the one-way sign pointing the wrong way and continued driving ahead instead of making the turn. The officer pointed out his error and told Bill he couldn't issue him a license until he learned to obey the law, that when a policeman gave orders, not following them was equivalent to violating the law. Bill walked away absolutely defeated; he never imagined he would fail; it was one more shove down the drain."

"Heck, Bill, why didn't you tell me what happened?"

Bill did not respond to the question, and another period of silence followed.

"If someone could have been with him in his dejected state, it might have made a difference. On the way home from the police station your mother lectured him that driving was a privilege, that earning a license through struggle gave it an additional value. On arrival, your mother dropped him, saying she had errands to do. Thus, Bill was left alone for several hours while his simmering anger grew. Although destroying household furnishings was not a good solution, perhaps Bill felt that it was the only way to get a human response."

Steve was silent for several minutes, then began, "What did it accomplish? What good did it do? Bill, I want to tell you something. As far as I'm concerned the most important thing is for you to get involved with people, develop your skills, and become a happier person. I wouldn't care if you broke everything in the house if that would really do it, but we both know it won't. *(Pause)* I wish you'd trust me and talk with me when you're in a jam. I want to help you." Steve looked directly at his brother and waited. *(Long pause)*

Bill slowly sat up in his chair, and with downcast eyes he turned toward Steve. Haltingly, but definitely, the words came. "I do trust you. I know it was wrong to break those things. But you don't understand. Getting a driver's license—that was my freedom, my chance to get away from them. Now I'm stuck. *(Pause)* That policeman was a fink. He deliberately tricked me. My driving was perfect right up to the last. He wanted me to fail. I could tell."

Steve interrupted: "Why didn't you talk with him after the test? Why didn't you tell him how you felt? It might have made a difference."

"I guess I was too mad to talk, and worried, too."

"Then why didn't you talk with me?"

"I thought you were with *them*. *They* wanted me to fail that test. They were glad. Besides, you weren't around when I got home. You don't know how awful I felt—cold inside and I—uh—a thought kept repeating itself over and over in my head: 'You're a failure. You're a failure. You're a failure.' I didn't care what happened to me and no one else was interested. At first, I tried pounding a pillow in my room but that didn't help. I got more and more nervous and restless. I paced back and forth. I felt just like I did when I went to that private school." *(Pause)*

"I understand, Bill. You felt totally abandoned."

"Yes, just like at Franklin. You could drop dead there and it wouldn't matter to anyone. No one cared.

I felt like a stranger; everyone was busy with their own affairs; they used to walk right by without seeing me. I wish I could explain to you what it was like. Everyone else was doing well and I was doing nothing. Everyone else was successful and I was a failure. I got so agitated, I ended up taking those tranquilizers. I felt cold and empty day after day—just awful. So I broke out and came back home."

Steve interruped again: "Bill, there are a lot of hard knocks in life. You've got to stay in there and fight. Don't give up so easily."

"I can stay and fight if somebody is interested, if somebody cares, if I know people like me, but when I'm miserable and they don't even know I exist, then I can't take it. Then nothing means anything. In that school, I found myself sweating and getting scared and wanting to run. I stayed as long as I could, but I was falling apart. At home, I was sweating too, angry that I had just been wiped out and everyone went on as if nothing had happened."

"Okay, okay. I could have been more responsive, but you also could have helped. *(Pause)* Will you promise me that if something is *that* wrong again you'll call me wherever I am?"

"I don't like to bother you. I know you get busy. You have your own friends and interests."

"But I want to help. I want you to interrupt me. You are important to me, Bill. Call me or find me if you ever get that angry and depressed again."

"I'll think about it. If I don't call you, I'll go off by myself somewhere and work it out. I won't smash or break anything again."

"Okay, be the strong, silent type then—at least that's better than being destructive."

A gradual change in the emotional climate had occurred—an easier, more comfortable exchange was taking place. The major issue separating the boys had been settled, and they were talking together, really listening with mutual respect. Although I still sensed a degree of reservation in Bill as he spoke to his brother, it seemed clear that the dispute had been settled. Bill held back, fearful of giving himself wholly to this relationship, fearful he would be hurt again. At the same time, there was warmth in his feeling for his brother, genuine regard and hunger for companionship. Obviously, Bill needed a great deal of reassurance and many, many positive experiences to overcome the damage of being so often a failure and a misfit.

Steve was smiling now, invitingly, and Bill was almost directly facing his brother, not quite with a smile but with a look of appreciation and warmth. In the next moment, the climate changed.

"Bill, why don't you try harder in school? Why don't you study more? The way you're going you may not even graduate. You'll end up doing something you don't want to do."

"You don't understand, Steve. I do try, I study real hard, and it doesn't make any difference. I even tried an experiment. I studied three hours every night for a month, and when I took the exams, I failed two of them and got a low grade in the third. I gave up. It was hopeless. I don't know what's wrong. Nothing I do works, and I get no help from my teachers."

"Bill, that's a defeatist attitude. I know some teachers are hard to get along with, but the way to win them over is to stay after class, or if they have a few minutes during class, tell them you're in trouble and need extra help. Most teachers are willing to cooperate with you if you cooperate with them."

"Not in that school. I hate those teachers."

"Look, Bill, I went to the same school. Those teachers are human, too. If you resent them and fight them, they'll fight back."

"I've had problems since the first grade. Miss Wilkins picked on me all the time and she spread gossip around the school that I was lazy. My reputation has followed me ever since."

"You know what I think, Bill. You're much too sensitive. You get upset about little things. My advice to you is settle down, get busy, and ignore the disagreements. If it's really important, make an issue of it. Otherwise, forget it, because it's ruining your life."

"I can't forget it; I can't stop thinking about what happened or what will happen. I don't want to go back to the same school. The teachers are against me and I don't have a chance."

"You sound pretty mixed up to me, Bill. I don't believe all those teachers are against you. I think you're against yourself. You dwell too much on little irritations."

"Not little irritations. They make nasty remarks, poke fun at me, and enjoy making me the butt of their jokes. They'd do anything to make me squirm."

"Who, Bill? Which ones? I think you've got it in for one or two teachers and you're exaggerating."

At this point, Bill responded in a confused way. He mentioned a number of teachers, started to talk further about them, and his voiced trailed off. It was difficult to know whether he was speaking of current teachers or teachers from earlier grades. He became increasingly distressed as Steve forced him to defend himself. Steve saw that his brother had become disorganized and withdrawn. After another long period of silence, Steve suggested that we bring the meeting to a close. Since I wanted to schedule a time with Bill, I asked him to remain.

Steve paused directly in front of Bill. "I'll wait for you upstairs. Give you a lift home."

Somewhat angrily, Bill answered, "Don't bother. I'll go by bus."

"What's wrong with you anyway. Why should you take a bus when you can have a free ride home."

Sarcastically, Bill responded, "I don't want a *free* ride. I've got the money, I'll pay my way."

Steve, sharply: "Suit yourself. If that's the way you want it—good-bye!"

"Wait a moment, Steve. Right now you're both demonstrating what you've been discussing the last two hours. Bill wants to go home with you but he wants to be sure you want him. Not just a "free" ride, in other words, charity, but a real invitation."

Bill interrupted, saying to me: "Forget it!" Then to Steve: "I'm taking the bus. I don't need anybody. I'm perfectly able to get home on my own."

"For a moment there, Bill, you really got to me. I almost went off in a huff. But I don't care what you say. I'm waiting for you upstairs and you're going home with me."

Not quite so strongly, tentatively, Bill answered: "I'll take the bus."

"Like hell you will. It's not just to give you a lift, you supersensitive character. It's because I don't want to leave here without you. I want to ride with you. I enjoy your company. *(Pause)* I'm waiting for you, Bill, no matter what you say."

Bill did not answer but had lowered his head noticeably and was struggling with his feeings. Steve paused a few moments in the tense atmosphere; then he walked out the door, waving to me and saying to Bill, "I'll see you upstairs." He closed the door as he went. The moment the door was closed, Bill burst into tears. Sobbing painfully, and with great difficulty, his words came.

"I've been lonely all summer long—so terribly lonely. I don't think I've ever been more alone. At times it seems that nobody—nobody is interested or cares what happens to me." (This was followed by several minutes of heavy sighing and weeping.)

"Steve was really inviting *you,* Bill, not just offering a stranger a ride. It's very clear to me that he enjoys being with you."

"I know that's true, but why can't I accept him? *(Pause)* All summer long I've been alone. I'm always in the wrong place at the wrong time. When people want me to be with them, I'm not around, or I feel so miserable I don't want to be with anyone. When I look for someone to be with, they're always busy. Nothing works for me. *(Pause)* Everytime I do something wrong there are always people around to tell me about it. I may do things right ninety-nine times and nobody notices, but the first mistake I make is quickly pointed out. I feel so—*miserable*. *(Beginning to weep again.)* Sometimes I think 'What's the use, I'm a complete failure.' *(Pause)* You must get awfully tired of my problems. *(Pause)* Someday I'll come in here and shock you by talking only about all the good things in my life. *(Pause)* I guess I'll go up and join Steve now. So long, and thanks for everything."

Bill reached out, his eyes glistening; he shook my hand. He stood shaking my hand firmly, affirmatively, for several moments, then, quickly he waved and moved out the door.

I realized in this meeting how complicated open communication can become—how easy to twist and entangle compassion, respect, filial love, and human rights into masks of pride, rivalry, deceit, and distrust; but once the barriers to communication are cast away, the flow of life and its return engender a new spirit of communion, inviting and real.

In the months following this interview, serious problems continued to arise in Bill's relations with others, but there was much more joy, spontaneity, and animation—much more the feeling that, for the most part, life was worthwhile. The brothers have kept their bond of friendship. The conflict that might have ended the relationship was resolved in the extended interview.

There is so much in life to disturb even the strongest roots of companionship; one violent episode, one betrayal can start a chain reaction. The confrontation is one way to counteract the chain reaction. A climate can be created in which the persons involved can face the conflict, thrash it out, and eventually return to a basic feeling of camaraderie and love.

CHAPTER 7

The Burden of Sensitivity and Compassion

In this chapter, I will explore my contacts with a seven-year-old girl who experienced a growing dread of her teacher and a mounting fear of school, which culminated in a convulsive disorder. The factors contributing to the crisis and the significant conditions in Karen's world will be briefly described and discussed.

In the hours of play therapy with Karen and in talks with her parents, the world in which Karen lived gradually emerged. Three centers of pressure created a feeling of helplessness and terror in Karen, the severest of which was Karen's contacts with her first grade teacher. The pattern of her school life is reflected in the following incident, which Karen described in one of our conversations.

> Mrs. Brooks was always yelling and getting mad at us. When she jumped on Peter she scared me. Peter sat next to me in school and she came screaming at him. Her face was ugly. She shook him and shouted, 'Peter I told you to listen when I pronounce the words didn't I? You aren't listening, are you Peter? You're stupid! You belong in kindergarten with the other babies. This is no place for you; you're wasting our time. Now go put your face against the wall for the rest of the reading period.'

Each morning, as Karen got ready for school, she

would feel a vague, violent dread, which increased to a point of terror when Karen imagined the consequences of being the next victim of her teacher's angry outbursts. Only with much effort and strain could she bring herself to take the steps that would take her to the doors of the school. Increasingly, Karen found it difficult to concentrate, to listen, and to relate to others. She became convinced that she was stupid and that one day she would make a mistake that would cause her teacher to spring upon her.

In her concern for others, Karen absorbed considerable grief. Each time she witnessed brutality, each time she saw distorted faces and shaking bodies, she cringed a little more. She had the strong feeling that the eyes of her teacher were always watching her, judging her, and waiting for the proper moment to accuse. Karen wanted to escape, yet she saw no exit, no way out of her awful predicament. In her imaginings and fantasies, she began to create macabre tales, and out of them a new form of terror, waking, screaming, and shaking uncontrollably in the middle of her nightmares.

She came to feel that she was guilty and saw herself on trial for every classroom misdemeanor. Increasingly, her world became tightened. She was convinced that she was doomed to suffer a severe punishment. It was only a matter of time.

In addition to fears and nightmares, Karen began to experience physical illness, nausea, and dizziness in school and on the way to school. She felt she was under surveillance, and the terror of this feeling spread until she was afraid to speak of it at all. She remained quiet at school, frozen in a private world of enormous fear.

At home, Karen tried to talk with her parents, to tell them that she was afraid of her teacher—terribly, terribly afraid. But they would not listen. They thought that she complained unnecessarily and that her stories

---

[1] Reprinted, with revisions, from Psychotherapy: Theory, Research and Practice, Vol. 1, No. 2, January 1964.

were exaggerated. When she complained of illness in the morning, they would not permit her to remain at home. The nightmares bothered them, but only enough to control the kinds of programs she watched on television. She was forced to continue in a school situation where she felt increasingly disabled and defenseless. She felt her parents did not listen to her or understand her. She began to slip away from the life at home into a world of frightening images, of ghosts and witches, of knives and blood and broken bones.

When the tension and fear reached an unbearable point, the dreaded encounter between Karen and her teacher occurred. Mrs. Brooks understood that "something strange was happening to Karen," but she did not know what or why. I have paraphrased Mrs. Brooks' description of the crisis and Karen's retelling of it into one account of the day Karen's world of fear crashed in on her.

Mrs. Brooks was explaining a lesson in the workbook. Suddenly, she stopped. Her eyes focused tightly on Karen. She took several steps toward her. Their eyes met for a moment. Karen stood up. Her entire body stretched. Her arms extended upward and a look of absolute alarm passed over her face. She began spinning and spinning until each person in the room revolved with her. This was it! The grave moment had come. She was experiencing an all-encompassing panic. Just as her teacher reached her, Karen lost consciousness. She slumped over her desk, making weird, grotesque, agitated body movements, convulsive motions of her muscles. She was having a brain seizure.

Karen was taken to a nearby children's hospital for a complete analysis of the convulsive disorder. Thorough laboratory and medical tests over a two-day hospitalization revealed completely negative results. There was no physical basis for the convulsion. The physician concluded that it was caused by extreme muscular tension, which he believed had been induced by psychic tensions and fears. He recommended that Karen not return to school until she had seen a child psychotherapist.

For the first time, Karen's parents realized that her fear of school had a reality basis. They knew now that they had contributed to her illness by not listening to her, by not being sympathetic and supportive when she tried to express her extreme reactions to school. They had thought that her physical complaints were dramatic gestures for getting attention and attempts to evade school. They had not understood the grave crisis Karen faced. They had not been a part of her private world of thought and feeling simply because they were too involved in their own expectations and goals. When they understood, they realized they had become strangers to Karen. They wanted to know her in her real feelings and perceptions and to understand her as an individual.

The third center of pressure in Karen's world was her neighborhood. Her parents were in conflict with the patterns of living in the neighborhood. They held to principles of individual rights and peaceful group life in a segregated community on the fringe of the city, in a marginal area where homes were substandard and rapidly disintegrating. It was an unstable, transient community, with a congested population and extremely limited space. There were no parks, playgrounds, or recreational areas in the immediate vicinity. The delinquency rate was high. Fighting in the streets, loud night quarrels, and battles with the police were frequent occurrences. Karen was often frightened by knife fights she had witnessed. At times, other children tried to provoke her into fighting. Some brandished knives before her and threatened her. She would run into her house and would withdraw for hours in fear. Once she saw a child in front of her house covered with blood and being taken away by an ambulance. She could still hear the shrill sirens when she related the experience. Through and through, Karen was a pacifist, verbalizing her conviction that fighting was wrong and could only harm people. She often asked why people could not live peacefully, why they wanted to hurt each other, why they hated rather than loved each other. She lived in a community of hovering violence and tragedy. Her extremely sensitive ways and her acute perceptiveness brought her daily anguish and unhappiness.

Since there was a delay in Karen's initial meeting with her therapist, her father, an elementary school teacher, decided to attempt a new approach with her. He studied a number of books on child guidance, took a graduate course in methods of counseling, and discussed therapeutic procedures with his wife. He began, in a simple way, to apply therapeutic principles and procedures in some of his contacts with Karen. Each day, he reserved a period of time to be alone with her. At these times he gave Karen his complete attention. He encouraged her to express her feelings and to share with him her wishes and fears, her hopes and desires, her interests and attitudes. Following these meetings, he sat quietly by himself, thinking through the moments with Karen, recapturing their conversations, attempting to understand the nature and meaning of Karen's existence. He kept a journal of some of these conversations. Several excerpts have been selected to convey the nature of the new, developing relationship between Karen and her father.

On one occasion, as Karen's father sat nearby while she bathed, the following conversation took place:

> K: I'm going to tell you a secret. I might as well tell you, Daddy. *(Pause)* I've got a secret. When you put me to bed, sometimes you spank me. I laugh. I wait until you're gone. When I know you're downstairs, then I laugh.
>
> F: Like this: HA! HA! HA!
> K: Just laugh. You don't hurt me.
> F: Funny daddy.
> K: Yeah.
> F: You know I never mean to hurt you.
> K: Yeah. I know.

On another occasion, Karen and her father came into conflict over her bedtime. An argument had been under way for several minutes when Karen began to cry. In a highly emotional voice, she protested the inconsistency between her parents and referred to her mother's promise.

>K: Mother said I could stay and watch until I got tired. And now you say I can't.
>F: When is that? How long do you want to watch?
>K: Until I get tired.
>F: That's just what you said before, until you got tired. I don't think that's a good idea.
>K: But Mommy promised. And now you say . . . *(Karen cries loudly.)*
>F: I know, but Mommy and I never discussed this. You can go watch TV, but if you don't decide to go to bed at a reasonable time then . . .
>K: How long?
>F: You watch until I come down unless you tire before then. But when I come downstairs, I'm going to say, "Karen, you're going to bed now and that's that! Do you understand?"
>K: Yes. *(After about half an hour, Karen, on her own, approaches her father.)*
>K: Daddy, I'm getting tired now. See my eyes, they're sleepy aren't they?
>F: Yes. You're ready. Up we go.
>Karen kisses her father.
>F: I'm so glad I have you.
>K: M-m-m.
>F: I love you when you're bad and I love . . .
>K: Love me when I'm good. *(Father takes Karen up to bed.)*

In another meeting with her father, Karen explores her troubled feelings.

>F: You look so unhappy, Karen. What's the matter?
>K: I don't know.
>F: Why don't you like yourself? Why don't you like Karen?
>*(Long pause)*
>K: I'm so dumb.
>F: You? Dumb?
>K: Yeah. I can't read.
>F: *(Emphatically)* You are not dumb and you read well.
>*(Long pause)*
>K: I'm so . . . *(Pause)*
>F: So . . . what?
>K: In—con, I can't pronounce it.
>F: Inconsiderate?

> K: Yes. Inconsiderate to everyone.
> F: Karen, you are not dumb. You read as well as most children. And you love us and we love you . . . and even if you were dumb or inconsiderate, which you are not, I'd still love you.
> K: Daddy, I love you too.

Karen continues to explore her feelings with her father. She reveals strategies she has used to manipulate her parents.

> K: Sometimes I purposely fall or hurt myself just to get attention.
> F: That's a hard way. Hurting yourself to get sympathy.
> K: No, to get attention.
> F: That's the hard way.
> K: I know a better way to get attention.
> F: How?
> K: By bothering you, pushing you . . .
> F: Yes?
> K: Sometimes I even want you to whip me. Then I can go to somebody and she'll stay with me and hug me and kiss me and let me stay up. But when you really hurt me and it stings, I lay there and call you names and feel like whipping you with nine whips like they use on horses.
> F: When you're looking for attention, couldn't you just tell us what you want instead of using all these angry ways?
> K: I guess I could.

In this final excerpt, Karen and her father are lying side by side. They have been together for a long while. Then, as Karen looks out the window, she begins to speak.

> K: I'm looking at the trees. They teach people a lesson.
> F: What do they teach you, Karen?
> K: The leaves are their lips and with their branches they look up to God and God sees them and helps them.
> F: Where did you learn that, Karen?
> K: I don't know. *(Pause)* Ride me downstairs now.
> F: Okay.

These private meetings between Karen and her father paved the way for the therapy that followed. In these meetings a process had begun in which Karen became increasingly open with her parents. A climate was created in which her parents really shared her struggles. A pattern of relating was evolving in which the individuality and uniqueness of Karen and her need for recognition were valued and given opportunity for expression.

Even so, Karen was still an easily frightened child. When she arrived for her first hour of therapy, she was withdrawn and evasive. She needed to be reassured again and again that in the playroom she was free to do what she wanted. She needed to be supported to make decisions that made sense to her. It was necessary to reaffirm that the toys and materials were there for her and that no one would interrupt us. Slowly she came to realize that I would be with her, to listen, to speak, to enable her to face her conflicts and fears, to enable her to express herself openly. It was obviously a new situation for Karen, a situation in which she did not need to seek attention and recognition because an adult was always in attendance and present for her.

She entered the first time in a quiet, frightened way, a stranger in a new setting, suspicious and distrustful. She looked around the room, evading me and seeking a spot in a corner of the sandbox. With her back to me, slowly she began to finger the sand. She remained in this way for the entire hour, afraid to face me, afraid to face the situation, restricting herself to the sandbox and to idle movements that seemed to comfort her by helping her to avoid the new experience. Only once did she look in my direction, and then but fleetingly. Obviously, Karen needed more time to take the first step toward an expanding self, more time to overcome the fear of the stranger in herself and the stranger in me. The apparently random motions in the sandbox were made over and over again. But there was one definite, observable change. The tension in her body disappeared; the agony of the beginning minutes was gone.

Our first hour came to a close with only one moment of direct communication. But the silence we shared was not unpleasant or without meaning. As Karen left, her eyes were smiling. The quiet, serene atmosphere, the patient waiting, the adult's concern and constant presence, the freedom engendered were all beginning to create a climate in which Karen could discover new regions within herself, new directions to enrich her life with others, and new resources for realizing her potentialities. The silence we shared in this hour was a way of living, a peaceful way that Karen had not often known. Respecting her and her readiness for a new life, her way of emerging in accordance with her own timetable, gave her the conditions she needed to explore her world and to develop more fully as a real self.

So I waited for Karen to act. I waited for her to make decisions. I waited for her to take the first step toward a new life. When she did, the shift was not a slow, gradual process but rather sudden and dramatic. Once she understood the nature of our meetings, once she internalized the values involved within the consistent structure of the relationship, Karen began to trust, to be spontaneous, to express and explore her world, and to share this expanding world with me.

In the second interview, the range of activity spread as did her use of the toys and materials. She initiated conversations with me. At one point, she spilled water on the floor and seemed considerably upset. She looked at me and waited for the criticism or punishment. When I made no comment, she hurried to get a sponge and wipe it up.

> CM: In here, if you spill and mess, it is all right . . . as long as you don't mind, it doesn't bother me.

Karen returned to the sandbox, mixing sand and water. Drops of water spilled on the floor. Momentarily, she looked in my direction; then she continued her play. She spilled a little of the wet sand on her dress. She looked at me and suddenly began to laugh, loudly.

> CM: In here you can laugh about messing. But what about at home.
> K: No. There I have to keep clean.

THE BURDEN OF SENSITIVITY AND COMPASSION

> CM: Your mother doesn't like you to get dirty.
> K: When I play with mud, I keep away from my mother. I try to wash it off before she sees me, but sometimes she catches me and screams K-A-R-E-N.
> CM: So, at home, there are some things your mother doesn't like you to do?
> K: Yes, many things.
> CM: You are not always free to do what you want to do.
> K: NO. Not free.

Karen really came to life as she talked of her relationship with her mother. Enthusiastically, she stirred water into the sand, mixed it, and sang: "Lots of water, loads of sand, first sand, then water. Scoop it and scoop it many different ways. But only one way to get dirty. Only one way. Dirty is dirty. Look, now you are a mess. And I don't care. Here we go again."

Later in the interview, while punching "Bobo," Karen began to talk in a low voice.

> K: I punch you some more. *(punches silently several times.)* You are not fast enough. You are too slow. *(The punching becomes harder, more frenzied.)* Again and again I tell you. You don't do what I say. *(The punching continues. Karen is conversing with "Bobo.")* You don't listen to me. You better pay attention. You'll see. You'll see.

The conversations continued to the end of the hour. As she played, Karen described her school experiences of the previous year. It was obvious that there was strong feeling against her teacher, but after a lengthy expression of feelings and after relating the incidents leading up to the final collapse and removal from school, her feelings began to change. "Mrs. Brooks had forty-three children to teach and that's a big job." Sometimes we wouldn't listen to her and she had a right to be mad at us." "I don't believe she wanted to hurt me or anyone. She wanted to frighten us so we would learn."

Shortly after Karen began her experience in therapy, a plan was evolved with her parents to place her in a private school, where pressures for academic achievement were at a minimum, where she would be a member of a small group in which individual differences were respected, where she could proceed to develop skills and knowledge at her own pace. The private school turned out to be an ideal placement in which Karen created a new image of teachers and schools. Within six weeks she had developed a new concept of herself in school. She became confident in her reading and arithmetic abilities. Her achievement was so much higher than any other child in the group that she became an assistant teacher, where her unusual sensitivity, her wish to help, and her understanding that learning can be difficult enabled her to assist other children to increased knowledge and skill and to new attitudes about themselves as learners.

She often spoke excitedly about incidents that occurred in the new school. One day she painted a picture of her school. In a happy voice she said, "I like my new school. I like my teacher. She's nice. She lets me help the other kids when they need help." Another time she said, "We have fun in our school. My teacher showed me how to make funny faces with clay. We call it modeling clay. We laugh at the faces we make."

The inner freedom to be, the confidence and spontaneity of the self were evident in all of the remaining interviews, through the final one, seven months later, when Karen decided she would no longer come for our meetings in the playroom. Many factors in combination contributed to the new developing sense of self and self-esteem: the parents' concern for Karen and their willingness to devote time and talent to develop deeper bonds and deeper understandings with her; the new teacher, who perceived Karen as a unique person, allowing her to proceed at her own rate, and giving her special opportunities to form helping relations with other children; and the therapy itself, where she could live openly, autonomously, and freely, but still within the framework of a relationship and a structure.

In the playroom, Karen related to the toys and materials. She spoke to the different items as she worked with them. There was always a gentle, tender concern for the material. I have selected one excerpt to illustrate the meaningful nature of Karen's relationship with the play materials.

Karen had procured a large piece of wood and several tools. She began to saw the wood.

> K: Oh wood! Oh wood! How you hurt when I saw you. But I'll make you into something new and something good. *(She continues to talk in this way until she saws the board in half.)* Now I'll nail you together. Wait, this nail is going in crooked. Oh, I'll have to take you out. Now stand straight until I get you in. *(Pause) (Tries again but fails.)*
> K: I'm losing my patience.
> CM: But you don't want to quit.
> K: No, but I'm losing my temper.
> CM: Then you will be in a jam.
> K: But I want to do it. Come on now. What's wrong? Is it you or is it me? *(Keeps working)* There, I got you. I got you right in. Ha! Ha! Ha! Ha! Now I'll put in your brother and see what happens.

Karen became involved in a variety of self-chosen activities. She used clay to cook meals, which she served to us. The meals were cooked her way, by her own recipes. She often exclaimed, "This is fun. This is really fun." She spoke of the delicious pies, cakes, and jellies her grandmother made for her, saying, with an ecstatic look on her face, "I love her food!"

Sometimes she played with the family figures. Occasionally, she scolded them or spanked them or isolated them in different parts of the room, as in the following sequence.

Karen takes a father, mother, sister and baby figure. One by one she examines them. She twists the bodies.

> K: Look I can twist these. Father is a big guy.

Karen continues to twist the figures. She scolds each family member as she sets the father, mother, sister, and baby precariously on top of a wall of the play house. Then she topples them over one by one. The "sister" begins to cry.

> K: She is crying. She is unhappy when they fight.
> CM: She doesn't like them to fight.
> K: No! Stop! Stop fighting!
> CM: She becomes very sad when they fight.
> K: They shouldn't fight. They shouldn't ever fight. They should always be friends.

Many times in her play Karen used items to express aggressive feelings, chiefly the "Bobo" and a ping-pong rifle. Karen also related to the rifle as a friend. When she shot the balls through the rifle, it was in the nature of a playful game. A few times she used a wooden lion or tiger as her target, but usually she shot aimlessly around the room, not caring where she shot or how she shot, not choosing a target but enjoying the feeling of shooting and the whole process of conversing with the rifle, loading it, and listening to the popping sounds of the balls as they came out.

As my meetings with Karen progressed, more and more she turned to painting and drawing and to reading books either silently or aloud to me. There were occasional times when she read silently the entire hour or when she painted quietly the whole time. It was good just to be present with her, to see her completely relaxed and contented, to see her totally absorbed in activity, and to find joy in being involved.

Her drawings and paintings were generally nature scenes. She made "soft, white snow" and "dancing clouds" and "fresh baby flowers." During these moments, Karen would occasionally sing or speak with me.

> K: These are fresh baby flowers, like in my garden.
> CM: Do you tend the flowers?
> K: Yes. I do. *(Pause) (Karen sings as she paints.)*
> CM: You're in a happy mood today.
> K: Yeah. Everything is fine.
> CM: Not just here but at home.
> K: Yeah.
> CM: And at school.
> K: Yeah.
> CM: Everywhere.
> K: *(Smiles)* Yes! Everywhere.

THE BURDEN OF SENSITIVITY AND COMPASSION 107

At the end of three months in the private school, Karen's parents moved. In discussions with them, it was decided to try Karen in the public school in her new neighborhood. This decision was discussed with Karen in one of our meetings.

> CM: Perhaps your parents have talked with you about going to a new school.
> K: Yes. They have.
> CM: They decided they wanted you to return to a public school so you would be more a part of your own neighborhood and go to school with the kids near your new home.
> K: Yes. I've seen the school. It's only a short way from where we live.
> CM: Are you ready to make a change, to leave your school. You know you can take as much time as you need to make the transfer.
> K: I visited there one day and met the teacher. She was nice to me. She invited me in and I sat by the window. I saw some beautiful trees through the window.
> CM: Perhaps it will be hard for you to change schools. You've been so happy where you are. *(Pause)* Have you thought about when you would like to make a transfer? *(Long pause)* Perhaps in a week or two?
> K: This week.
> CM: But there are only two days left.
> K: I'll tell my friends good-bye tomorrow.
> CM: Okay. I'll call Mr. Jensen, the principal of your new school, and see if you can begin on Friday. If not, perhaps you could start Monday morning. I'll call you at home tomorrow and let you know.
> K: Okay.

For the next ten minutes Karen talked about school experiences, her teacher and her friends. She related a number of enjoyable events and activities. There was a wistful, sad quality in her voice.

> CM: A little sad to leave your school.
> K: Yes. *(Long pause)* *(Then Karen painted silently the rest of the hour.)*

In our next meeting, Karen spoke at length about her new school. She had already initiated a number of friendships. She enjoyed her teacher and the activities of the school. From her own statements, she was positively launched in her new community. Three months later, Karen brought her report card. She received four A's and two B's. It was shortly after this time that Karen decided to terminate the hours of therapy. Discussions with her parents confirmed my observation that for some months she had been growing in a spontaneous, creative way, developing her potentialities, establishing friendships, and broadening the scope of her interests and activities. The new neighborhood offered her a spacious world, with expanded recreational and human resources.

Our last meeting was a fascinating experience. The feelings conveyed during the many weeks that Karen played with the baby figures and the baby-puppets—the soft and tender concern—were brought to life, as an ongoing moment-by-moment reality, when Karen and her younger sister, Kathy, came together in the playroom. Karen was solicitous and helpful, but not dominating or restrictive. She made resources available and assisted when necessary, but she took her cues from Kathy. She was open, receptive, and invitational, not demanding or manipulating, not directing or controlling. All the way through the hour, she served Kathy in a beautiful, sensitive way, listening to her, standing by when needed, playing with her, and leaving her by herself once she was launched in an activity or project.

At one point, Karen sympathized with my dilemma, "Hard to listen to two people and keep your eyes and ears on both of them, isn't it?"

Karen painted as she talked to me.

> K: This is my last time here. I wanted to bring Kathy so she could have fun here like I have.
> CM: Yes, I know, Karen. *(Pause)* After today, on Wednesday afternoons, you'll play with your friends after school.
> K: Yes. But some days I'll probably say, "I wish I could go see Dr. Moustakas."
> CM: Perhaps you'll come for a visit.

(Karen finishes her painting and turns to me.)

K: Would you like to keep my painting? I made some birds, the sun and the sky, and some grass. I would like you to have it.

CM: Yes, I would like it, Karen. Thank you for thinking of me. *(Pause)*

K: How many children do you have coming here?

CM: Do you have any idea.

K: Maybe two dozen?

CM: Not that many, but quite a few. *(Pause)* But when you're here, you're the only one I have.

K: *(Looking at the clock)* Okay, Kathy, it's time for us to go now. Daddy will be waiting. So long, Dr. Moustakas. Thank you for letting me come here all these weeks.

CM: I'm glad to have met you, Karen. I hope you will continue to enjoy learning and having fun in school. Perhaps you'll come sometime again for a visit.

K: Goodbye!

CM: Goodbye, Karen.